TH

REVEALER

OF

THE
REVEALER
OF

HANK KUNNEMAN

Charisma
HOUSE
A STRANG COMPANY

Most STRANG COMMUNICATIONS BOOK GROUP products are available at special quantity discounts for bulk purchase for sales promotions, premiums, fundraising, and educational needs. For details, write Strang Communications Book Group, 600 Rinehart Road, Lake Mary, Florida 32746, or telephone (407) 333-0600.

THE REVEALER OF SECRETS by Hank Kunneman
Published by Charisma House
A Strang Company
600 Rinehart Road
Lake Mary, Florida 32746
www.strangbookgroup.com

Unless otherwise noted, all Scripture quotations are from the New King James Version of the Bible. Copyright © 1979, 1980, 1982 by Thomas Nelson, Inc., publishers. Used by permission.

Scripture quotations marked AMP are from the Amplified Bible. Old Testament copyright © 1965, 1987 by the Zondervan Corporation. The Amplified New Testament copyright © 1954, 1958, 1987 by the Lockman Foundation. Used by permission.

Scripture quotations marked CEV are from the Contemporary English Version, copyright © 1995 by the American Bible Society. Used by permission.

Scripture quotations marked KJV are from the King James Version of the Bible.

Scripture quotations marked THE MESSAGE are from *The Message: The Bible in Contemporary English*, copyright © 1993, 1994, 1995, 1996, 2000, 2001, 2002. Used by permission of NavPress Publishing Group.

Scripture quotations marked NCV are from The Holy Bible, New Century Version. Copyright © 1987, 1988, 1991 by Word Publishing, Dallas, Texas 75039. Used by permission.

Design Director: Bill Johnson
Cover design by Justin Evans

Library of Congress Cataloging-in-Publication Data:
Kunneman, Hank.
  The revealer of secrets / by Hank Kunneman. -- 1st ed.
    p. cm.
  ISBN 978-1-59979-775-5
  1. God (Christianity) 2. Revelation--Christianity. 3. Prophecies. 4. Dreams--Religious aspects--Christianity. 5. Visions. I. Title.
  BT127.3.K86 2009
  234'.13--dc22
                                        2009021472

This publication has been translated in Spanish under the title *El revelador de secretos*, copyright © 2009 by Hank Kunneman, published by Casa Creación, a Strang Company. All rights reserved.

10 11 12 13 14 — 10 9 8 7 6 5 4
Printed in the United States of America

This book is dedicated to the Holy Spirit and His prophets, who sacrificed and gave their lives to deliver the word of the Lord. Their words still speak today, and the sounds of their persecuted blood prophesy in every generation!

CONTENTS

ONE

HEARING THRONE-ROOM SECRETS

After these things I looked, and behold, a door standing
open in heaven. And the first voice which I heard was like
a trumpet speaking with me, saying, "Come up here, and
I will show you things which must take place after this."

—Revelation 4:1

I WAS USHERED INTO A ROOM TO FIND A VERY WELL-DRESSED, dignified-looking man standing there surrounded by security men. I had never met this man, nor did I know who he was. Someone standing next to me said, "This man would like for you to give him a word from God." I agreed, not knowing what to expect. I prayerfully put my hand upon his shoulder and waited to see if the Lord would speak anything to me. I opened my mouth, and the Lord began to reveal many secrets from this man's life, including some things about his future.

After a few minutes of speaking some very detailed things I heard from the Lord, I opened my eyes to see tears in his eyes and a look of shock on his face. I was shocked too! Then he explained who he was by saying, "I am the president of...," naming the nation. He went on to say, "I have sought psychics and others, but, sir, your words cause my bones to rattle. You have told me secrets no one knows, even regarding things on my desk."

This experience reminded me of what happened with Daniel when he interpreted a dream for King Nebuchadnezzar. Because the power of the Lord was upon Daniel's words, the king immediately knew that the dream was from God and that the Lord was indeed the King and Lord of all: "Truly your God is the God of gods, the Lord of kings, and a revealer of secrets, since you could reveal this secret" (Daniel 2:47).

Yes, God truly is the *Revealer of secrets*, as this verse affirms. This attribute of God will cause the highest leaders to bow to the Lord. I thank the Lord that I have had other great opportunities to minister to leaders and presidents of nations. It is a wonderful thing to see their touching responses as they hear what God wants to reveal to them.

In the Bible, God always had a prophetic voice that carried the secrets of the Lord to kings and leaders of nations. Still today, as Revelation 4:1 indicates, doors are being opened in heaven to receive throne-room secrets, and, at the same time, doors are opening in the earth for us to share these secrets, which show the heart and will of God for all people—even leaders of nations.

Throne-Room Secrets

When the Lord opened the door for me to receive throne-room secrets for the leader mentioned at the beginning of this chapter, it resulted in great blessings for him and his country. It is not uncommon for God to place a spokesman who has heavenly secrets in his or her mouth to minister to leaders. In fact, prophetic words should be a key element affecting nations in a positive way.

God used specific individuals in the Bible to change the course of history for certain nations. Two prophets, Nathan and Samuel, spoke to King David and helped his leadership. Throughout the books of 1 and 2 Kings, prophets or spokesmen for God spoke words to kings of nations to help them rule their nations. Leaders who listened to God's prophets and obeyed were always blessed with the rich rewards of God's blessings. Today, as then, it is vitally important for there to be prophetic voices who can speak—and leaders in the political arena who will listen—thus allowing nations who obey God's voice to step into God's blessing.

However, God's secrets are not just for the political realm. They are for us as individuals and for other people whom we will encounter. The Lord desires for us to see and hear what heaven is up to concerning us here on Earth. You can ask—and even expect—God to be the Revealer of secrets in your life.

PRINCIPLES FOR RECEIVING GOD'S SECRETS

In Isaiah 6 we see some very important principles we need to understand in order to receive the secrets of the Lord on any level, whether for the highest national leader or the average person's everyday life. Take a look at these principles from Isaiah 6:

1. "I saw the Lord" (verse 1)—If you are in position with God to hear throne-room secrets, you will get to see the Lord. It is important to recognize that you are representing God Himself and His character when you share what you believe He is saying. People must see only Jesus and His heart.

2. "Holy, holy, holy..." (verse 3)—This is what the prophet Isaiah heard the angels saying. Never forget that you are being entrusted with something holy, and it should be treated as such when you share the things you believe you have heard and seen. God's secrets should never come across pridefully, rudely, or unmannerly, nor should they be overspiritualized or delivered with unnecessary drama.

3. "Woe is me, for I am undone" (verse 5)—God wants to change you and prepare you to share His heart. To be changed, you have to be willing to see your shortcomings and deal with them. When you decide to change and desire to become like Christ, then you can be trusted with the deep secrets of God's heart.

4. "I am a man of unclean lips…my eyes have seen…the LORD" (verse 5)—Once you recognize that the Lord is the only One deserving any credit, you gain the right to speak for Him. Many want to share His secrets, but they take their eyes off Jesus and seek the attention and applause of those to whom they speak instead. We are simply earthen vessels. Place your eyes on Him until you want only Him to receive all the glory.

5. "One of the seraphim…having in his hand a live coal…touched my mouth with it" (verses 6–7)—God wants to refine your words and your methods of delivering them, and He wants to teach you the art of knowing when to share and when to keep silent. God uses a spiritual coal to refine your words. When you do speak, you will speak exactly what the Lord wants in a statesmanlike way. It is important to learn discipline with the word of the Lord. Not everything we may see or hear from heaven's throne is meant to be shared, or it may have a specific timing for being shared.

6. "Go, and tell" (verse 9)—Here we learn obedience. You should always remember that "Go, and tell" comes *after* you experience the things that first build your character. In addition, no matter what God asks, you must be obedient to deliver His word—even if it is something you don't want

to do. For example, you cannot run from the assignment of God the way Jonah did when he tried to avoid going to Nineveh.

These principles have helped me when I share the word of the Lord to people. My most important motive must always be to lift up Jesus and represent myself correctly in all that I share. I have come to realize that the more I am changed and walk as Jesus did, the more correctly I can share His words to others.

I remember one particular time when I had to be obedient to share a throne-room secret that didn't look like it was going to come to pass. Back before the election of 2000, God had opened up a throne-room secret that I felt strongly directed to share. I shared it with many around the United States. Literally, the Lord showed me that George W. Bush was going to be the next president of the United States. I knew in my heart that this word from God must not be clouded by my own political interpretation, endorsement, preference, or opinion. Instead, I was being trusted with what the Lord was saying would come "after this" (Revelation 4:1).

I knew the importance of keeping my preferences from being a factor in what I was seeing about President Bush because previously, during the nineties, the Lord had shared another secret regarding the presidential election of Bill Clinton. He had shown me that Clinton would be elected president, and I had to prophesy this to the disappointment of many Christians. My opinion could not get in the way of the secret given to me. In fact, in that earlier election, I even voted for someone else in spite of what I prophesied!

THE VISION OF THE HAND

I soon discovered that I would be tested in my heart regarding the word I had received regarding the election of President Bush. When election day arrived, although I shared this word with many people, it appeared that the opposite was actually happening! "The president of the United States is Al Gore," said the news station that I was listening to the night of the 2000 election. I remember how I felt when I heard it. "What! How could this be?" I thought. I wanted to pull the blanket over my head as I lay in bed recounting the many people who heard me proclaim the secret I believed to be from God.

I had seen a vision in December 1999 and then again in June 2000 while ministering in a conference during which God revealed His word to me. I saw a dark hand being raised up over the United States from the soil of the earth. Something was being held inside its palm. The hand grew taller and taller as it pushed up from the earth. Then I noticed a brilliant shaft of light above the earth, coming from the direction of the heavens toward the United States, where the hand was. Inside the dark hand was Al Gore. The hand was raising him up from the earth until the shaft of light pushed the hand holding Al Gore forcibly back to the earth until it disappeared.

The same heavenly shaft of light then began to move in a counter-clockwise motion three times. It reached down and raised up a man who stood in the midst of this light. The light placed the man over the White House. I recognized that the man was George W. Bush. As I look back now at this vision, I realize that God was showing me what was going to take place with the election—including even the three recounts of votes in Florida, indicated by the counterclockwise motion of the light three times.

So you can imagine how I felt that day when the opposite of what I had seen seemed to be happening. Eventually, however, to my relief, the vision did happen as I had seen it, but I had to be obedient to it even when it tested my confidence.

It is so important that the door to heaven is open today so we can hear what God wants to say and do in this generation. His word prepares us to be the mighty church for the tasks at hand. The day that we are living in was foretold in Daniel 12 as prophetic seals are being opened and End Time events are being made known:

> "But you, Daniel, shut up the words, and seal the book until the time of the end; many shall run to and fro, and knowledge shall increase."...Although I heard, I did not understand. Then I said, "My lord, what shall be the end of these things?" And he said, "Go your way, Daniel, for the words are closed up and sealed till the time of the end."
>
> —DANIEL 12:4, 8-9

God is reserving certain events and things for a specific time. These are not meant to be spooky revelations from some psychic, but rather a fulfillment of Scripture whereby God opens the door of heaven and we receive a glimpse of what the Lord wants to bring about. As a result of receiving God's revelations, we can be prepared to act accordingly.

Often when I have received a word from God about such an event, I did not understand or even like the outcome of what I saw and heard. For example, while ministering on December 14, 2003, in a vision I saw a fist coming and striking over Iran, and I heard the word *Bam*! I told the audience what I saw, but none of us knew what this meant, so all we could do was pray. Sadly, less than two weeks later, on December 26, a major earthquake happened in the city of Bam, Iran.[1] I wasn't really sure why God showed this to me, except to have us pray and perhaps prevent even more deaths from the horrific event. We may never know fully until we all reach heaven how our prayers helped that situation.

When we don't understand the purpose of what we see in the secrets of the Lord, it is vital that we just pray. Sometimes God will reveal even more information or a plan of action in prayer; at other times, He may not reveal more. In that case, keep covering the situation in prayer.

THE WORLD HAS HARD QUESTIONS

Things such as terrorism, violence, natural disasters, presidential elections, and other historical events are occurring everywhere, and the world is coming to us with hard questions. The Bible says in 2 Chronicles 9:1, "Now when the queen of Sheba heard of the fame of Solomon, she came to Jerusalem to test Solomon with hard questions." This is exactly where the world is today. They are wondering what heaven is up to and what God is saying. They are curious to know if God would, in fact, speak of such things.

The answer is *yes*! God always has a spokesman or prophet through whom He desires to reveal these types of secrets.

I want you to be encouraged that God has not left you on this planet without hope. Amos 3:7 says, "Surely the Lord GOD does nothing, unless He reveals His secret to His servants the prophets." The Bible also encourages us in Ezekiel 7:26: "Disaster will come upon disaster, and rumor will be upon rumor. Then they will seek a vision from a prophet." Wow! God has not left you and me without hope or a spokesman! Whether it is literal disasters or terrifying rumors, He will do nothing without first sharing His secrets.

We know this actually happened in the days of Abraham before the cities of Sodom and Gomorrah would potentially be destroyed. God went down to share His heart with His friend Abraham. "And the LORD said, 'Shall I hide from Abraham what I am doing?'" (Genesis 18:17). Here God came down to His friend Abraham to share a throne-room secret. This event concerning Sodom and Gomorrah could have been avoided had there been ten righteous people, according to the number Abraham suggested to the Lord. God was giving His friend an opportunity to be involved in stopping something that was about to happen. Just like people today, I am sure many people who lived back then wondered what in the world was going on after the cities were destroyed.

The questions of man are not getting easier, and God's desire to share

His secrets is becoming greater because He longs to share His heart and perspective with us as He did with Abraham. We must be ready when these very hard questions are asked. First Peter 3:15 says, "Always be ready to give a defense to everyone who asks you a reason for the hope that is in you, with meekness and fear."

This was especially true after the events of September 11, 2001. Many in the world did not have answers to the very difficult questions, and sometimes it seemed that there were not very many of God's spokesmen. It also seemed that not too many Christians even saw it coming—let alone knew what to say to the world after it happened.

I was one of those who felt caught off guard. The only thing I recall about it was that I had a dream the night before where I saw a building on fire, people screaming and holding hands, and some even jumping out of a building. There was no further understanding, interpretation, or instruction. I prayed about it for a few moments in the morning, but it wasn't until later when I heard the news that I had any clue about the dream. I really didn't see it coming enough to respond. Was the dream a warning and a call to pray?

I know from life's experiences as well as from the Bible that God doesn't show us everything all the time. If He did, we simply wouldn't be able to handle it emotionally. However, He will give us the answers we need to minister to the world in the time of need if we seek Him. But we should not feel that we have a responsibility to try to answer the questions for which God is not revealing His word to us.

Even though Elisha was a powerful prophet of the Lord, we see in 2 Kings that even this man of God did not know everything:

> And so she departed, and went to the man of God at Mount Carmel. So it was, when the man of God saw her afar off, that he said to his servant Gehazi, "Look, the Shunammite woman! Please run now to meet her, and say to her, 'Is it well with you? Is it well with your

husband? Is it well with the child?'" And she answered, "It is well."

—2 KINGS 4:25-26

We must never think that we have to know every prophetic secret. As the world presents hard questions to us, we must first realize that not any one person or prophet has all the secrets, as was the case of Elisha above. In this case, the prophet didn't know this woman's son had died.

Many prophets and prophetic people are afraid to say, "I don't know." They feel pressured to have all the revelation from God for everything, and this simply is not biblical. No one person or prophet has all the answers, and we must have the maturity to say so when we didn't hear anything from the Lord about a specific matter. People in the world will respect us more when we can honestly say that although we are not certain about a matter at the moment, we will continue to pray and allow God to show us what we need to know for that situation. This way we can better give the world legitimate answers from God's throne.

We see another important key about God's secrets in 1 Kings 19, where God told Elijah that there were seven thousand other prophets who didn't bow their knee and who could also hear His secrets. God was reminding His prophet that the focus was not all about Elijah. That mighty prophet didn't have all the answers—there were seven thousand others through whom God spoke. Don't allow yourself to feel pressured to have your finger on the prophetic pulse of every single matter. Realize that God uses many vessels, and in many situations He will reveal secrets to someone else instead of you. The key is to stay humble and available so God can reveal His secrets to you in His own way and in His own time.

Even when the secret of the Lord is revealed to us, there will be times when we won't quite understand what it means or even what might happen next. For example, how would you and I like to have the vision that Ezekiel had in Ezekiel 10 when he saw the wheel within the wheel?

Or how about the awesome responsibility of the apostle John on the island of Patmos when he saw the prophetic events found in the Book of Revelation? Wow! To this day, the Book of Revelation still remains somewhat of a mystery, and no one seems to have an exact interpretation of it. Imagine what it was like as John was receiving it!

Even if you don't understand the details, when you receive a word from God, just record it, pray about it, and wait until God brings further revelation, through either you or someone else. Remember, the secret is still needed even when we don't understand it. Otherwise, God wouldn't have given it!

THE LORD HAS HIDDEN HIS SECRET

I have had to learn that I may not understand every revelation when it comes. This was the case when I received the word regarding Bam, Iran, which I mentioned earlier. I had a specific revelation but didn't know what it meant. A similar thing happened in regard to September 11. The only thing I had about that was the brief dream about people jumping from a burning building, but I never related it to any pending disaster. I believe the Lord hid specific details about both events from my eyes as He did with Elijah in 2 Kings 4:27: "The man of God said, '…the LORD has hidden it from me, and has not told me.'"

Back in May 2004, while ministering in Florida, I prophesied about back-to-back hurricanes that would come that year. This prophetic secret was revealed just prior to the season when we saw all the hurricanes in Florida and the United States. These hurricanes happened later that year in August. Then on another occasion shortly after, I prophesied the name of a hurricane and the exact month it would come to Florida that year based on a dream I had. I guess people decided they didn't want another hurricane like the previous ones, and scores of people prayed and attacked that storm in prayer.

After these events, both before and after Hurricane Katrina came destructively to New Orleans, I received calls from people asking if God had spoken to me about it. I had to tell people that God did not reveal anything to me about Katrina as He had done with the others. This shocked some people, and others responded rudely to me, as if I should know every secret of the earth. I told them that the Lord had hidden it from my eyes.

Sometimes the most difficult thing to say is "I don't know" or "God hasn't shown me." It is when people feel pressured to give in to the demands of people and perform in order to please man that they get off track and outside the anointing. Jesus related this point best in Matthew 11 when He talked about the prophet John the Baptist. I like how *The Message* says it:

> When John's disciples left to report, Jesus started talking to the crowd about John. "What did you expect when you went out to see him in the wild? A weekend camper? Hardly. What then? A sheik in silk pajamas? Not in the wilderness, not by a long shot. What then? A prophet? That's right, a prophet! Probably the best prophet you'll ever hear. He is the prophet that Malachi announced when he wrote, 'I'm sending my prophet ahead of you, to make the road smooth for you.'"
> —MATTHEW 11:7–10, THE MESSAGE

When Jesus said, "What did you expect when you went out to see him?" it appears He was implying that the prophet John the Baptist didn't meet the disciples' standard or expectations for his performance. Were they expecting John to put on some great prophetic show? This mind-set can cheapen or cause us to miss what God is saying.

Such an expectation can pressure people to perform until they tell people what they want to hear rather than what God is actually saying. Prophets are of great importance to us and have a special place in the heart of God. However, even the most skilled prophets do not know everything and shouldn't be treated as though they do. They are human and can make mistakes. They can miss it or wrongly interpret the throne-room secrets they are given.

I have also seen on the flip side where it wasn't that the prophet failed to accurately give God's word, but those who were listening failed to correctly understand the interpretation because they were too focused on wanting to see some kind of prophetic show that fit what they wanted to hear. Because they weren't listening with *spiritual ears*, they blamed the spokesperson for *missing it*.

This is why Jesus said to be careful how you hear (Luke 8:18). His emphasis was *on hearing*. We will look at this more clearly in a later chapter.

Another point to consider is that God may give someone a prophetic word about an event related to one certain season, but He may never again give that person another prophetic word. For example, it appears that the prophet Jonah only received the word of the Lord about Nineveh. After that, you never hear about him again, nor do you find him speaking a word of repentance to another city! The New Testament tells us that we "know in part and we prophesy in part" (1 Corinthians 13:9). When God reveals part of a throne-room secret to you, you must hear just that part and measure it against the Word of God. The Word of God is always the highest measuring standard of any prophetic secret, and it will keep you accurate.

You may not find an exact chapter and verse that line up with the prophetic word you receive. However, the concept of what is being said and how it is being shared must line up with the principles of Scripture. When the word—and how it is delivered—aligns with the Bible, we can trust God's prophets and receive God's blessings!

> Jehoshaphat stood up and said, "Listen my friends, if we trust the LORD God and believe what these prophets have told us, the LORD will help us, and we will be successful."
>
> —2 CHRONICLES 20:20, CEV

Another common misconception regarding prophets or prophetic secrets is that prophets should not need to ask the individual to whom they are prophesying to give them any information about their situation because this will indicate that they are not anointed enough. They feel prophets should always *get their information from the Lord.*

At times when I am ministering, I find it helpful to ask people a question about their situation. This does not indicate a lack of prophetic revelation. A person receiving God's word may not hear certain pieces of information or may simply need further clarity on what he or she is hearing. Asking questions can help to discern the situation more correctly. This happened with the prophet Elijah when he met the widow woman whose son had died. Notice the questions he asked his servant to ask: "Is it well with you? Is it well with your husband? Is it well with the child?" (2 Kings 4:26).

Sometimes I will ask a question to confirm what I am sensing because I may not really know for certain what I am hearing from God. At other times, by asking a question I can discern that nothing specific is being revealed to me and that the Holy Spirit is not leading me to minister to that person about the specific thing he or she is asking me about.

On one particular occasion, a question I asked a woman in a church where I was ministering proved to be a great blessing. I heard the Lord say to me, "Tell that woman in the back that she lost her husband six months ago." After I received this word, I looked at the woman God directed me to. What I saw didn't seem to line up with the word that I had just heard. I saw a huge wedding ring on her left hand with a diamond as big as a stop sign! It was glowing as bright as the sun and taunting me! I thought, "How could she have lost her husband? She has this gargantuan ring!"

She was standing next to a guy about her same age, whom I assumed must have been her husband. Nevertheless, I went for it! Pointing in her direction, I said, "Lady in the back there, did you lose your husband six months ago?" As soon as I said that, she fell to the ground weeping! "Well, I must be right," I thought. "Now what?"

After a few minutes, she picked herself up from the floor and said, "Yes, that is correct!" I then went on to share a beautiful word for her life that may not have happened had I not asked her that question.

You might be saying, "Well, I have never heard the kinds of specific things that you mentioned." Be encouraged; I have met countless people who don't even consider themselves prophets, much less called to ministry, who have heard the kind of specific secrets I just mentioned. Anyone can hear secrets from the Lord if they will seek God for them.

God communicates to us in different ways, and He chooses certain spokesmen to hear and deliver specific secret words. The key for each of us to understand is this: God *will* use *you* to hear *some* of His secrets. God is always extending His arms and voice to us no matter what the situation is. However, if we are always too afraid to step out and try, we will miss out on the things God may want to say.

"HOW LONG WILL THE ENEMY MOCK YOU, O GOD?"

The condition of our day has brought many challenges, such as earthquakes, terrorism, war, crime, divorce, broken hearts, and broken dreams. It can leave us desperate and confused, wondering what God might be saying. We find ourselves saying things like, "What are You saying, Lord? Is there anyone who can speak to me?"

Many people feel this way today. My wife, Brenda, and I desperately want to teach and demonstrate God's secrets with sound biblical wisdom. The devil does not want us to hear the secrets of the Lord this way. Throughout history, the prophets of God have been silenced, stoned, and put to death because Satan knows the great effect the word of the Lord has in the earth!

Look at what the Bible says happens when there is no one available with whom God can share His secrets:

They said in their hearts, "We will crush them
   completely!"
They burned every place where God was worshiped in
   the land.
We are given no miraculous signs;
No prophets are left,
And none of us knows how long this will be.
How long will the enemy mock you, O God?
Will the foe revile your name forever?
                                   —PSALM 74:8–10, NIV

This sounds a lot like today, doesn't it? A land without the secrets of the Lord is what the devil is after! He wants to keep God and His people silent so evil will become the predominant voice and sound. In this way, the devil mocks God and His people. This mockery happens when there are no secrets revealed and no spokespeople or prophets of the Lord. In order to carry out his devilish plan, Satan makes people unsure and hesitant about asking the Lord to speak to them about the most important situations in the earth.

Another method the devil has used throughout the centuries is *religious tradition*, which asserts that God doesn't speak today through prophets. However, the Bible emphatically proclaims that God has given prophets to the church (Ephesians 4:11). Ephesians 2:20 proclaims that prophets are one of the foundation stones of the church. Look at 1 Corinthians 12:28: "God has appointed these in the church: first apostles, second prophets, third teachers, after that miracles, then gifts of healings, helps, administrations, varieties of tongues." It is God who *set* these ministries in the church. That has not changed.

You may not be called to the biblical office of a prophet, but you were created to prophesy. "Prophesy? Who, me?" you might be saying. Prophecy is not weird, spooky, or outdated. It is God sharing His heart with you and through you for either your own situation or for that of someone else. Prophecy is literally heaven's secrets given to us for a specific purpose. The Bible tells us what prophecy is and what it accomplishes in our lives: "He who prophesies speaks edification and exhortation and comfort to men" (1 Corinthians 14:3). Prophecies are secrets of the Lord revealed to build up, encourage, and comfort people. This is exactly what this earth needs in the midst of so much confusion, panic, fear, and hopelessness.

You don't have to be afraid of prophecy. In fact, God doesn't want us to despise prophesying or sharing the secrets of the Lord. First Thessalonians 5:20 says, "Do not despise prophecies." We just need to know how to recognize the secrets of the Lord and how to use the proper protocol when sharing them to bring the highest honor to our King, Jesus Christ.

THE SECRET KEY

Giving honor to the Lord is truly the greatest privilege that we can live for. It is an awesome privilege to share His secrets, and we must be prepared to do so properly. You may be asking, "How do I learn to share His secrets? How can I understand them? How can I rise to a new level of receiving His throne-room secrets?"

The verse we began this chapter with speaks of "a door standing open in heaven," through which a voice advises, "Come up here, and I will show you things which must take place after this" (Revelation 4:1). With that in mind, I want you to see some more verses from the Book of Revelation that offer some clues to the key we need to receive the throne-room secrets of God.

In Revelation 3:20, we read, "Behold, I stand at the door and knock. If anyone hears My voice and opens the door, I will come in to him and dine with him, and he with Me." Here we see the Lord standing at the door and waiting for us to spend time alone—something we must do in order to hear His voice and receive His throne-room secrets!

There is another important point in Revelation 3:7. Doors and keys go together. We learned of the "open door" in Revelation 4:1, and this verse identifies the specific key we should be using: "These are the words of him who is holy and true, who holds the key of David" (Revelation 3:7, NIV). It was not just any key; it was the key of David. What was significant about David? According to the Bible, David was a man after the heart of God (Acts 13:22), even though he did sinful things at times. He always worshiped God and sought to keep his heart right before the Lord. It was David's heartfelt, committed passion for the Lord that became known as a *key*. What key is it? It is the key to enter the door of God's throne, where we find His heart.

When we truly seek the heart of God, His secrets will be given to us. Remember that He stands knocking, and if we open our hearts, He will come and fellowship with us in such an intimate way that we will hear His voice! The primary key to the secrets of God is intimacy with Him, which comes from spending time with Him. The Lord stands and knocks. Will we respond? The greatest secrets given to us are found in our desire and pursuit of face-to-face encounters with Him.

Look at what God said about His servant Moses:

> And the LORD said to them, "Now listen to what I say:
> If there were prophets among you,
> I, the LORD, would reveal myself in visions.
> I would speak to them in dreams.
> But not with my servant Moses.
> Of all my house, he is the one I trust.
> I speak to him face to face,
> Clearly, and not in riddles!
> He sees the LORD as he is.
> So why were you not afraid
> To criticize my servant Moses?"
> —NUMBERS 12:6–8, NLT

From these verses we can identify four levels through which we may receive the throne-room secrets that God makes available to us today.

1. Entry level

> The LORD will come down upon Mount Sinai in the
> sight of all the people.
>
> —EXODUS 19:11

This first, or entry, level deals with the simple gift of prophecy. It's entry level because we can all prophesy (1 Corinthians 14:31). The people were at the bottom of the mountain when the Lord appeared. It is from there that you begin to hear from God. The secrets He reveals at this level are not necessarily specific in nature but are broader and are designed to build up and encourage the hearers.

In the nineteenth chapter of Exodus, God told Moses to set boundaries at the bottom of the mountain and God would visit them. Then when the people heard God's sound, it was in the form of thunder and lightning. In other words, it wasn't specific; they heard the Lord but in an unclear way.

Afterward, the people actually ran in terror from God's presence and voice. They told Moses, "You speak with us, and we will hear; but let not God speak with us, lest we die" (Exodus 20:19). This is how many feel when the Lord wants to speak. They are terrified! They would rather have someone else hear from God and give them God's specific words for fear of making a mistake if God spoke directly to them. They would rather hear God in the general things, where it sounds like a thunderous noise and presents the same general sound for all who might be nearby. They don't feel confident to hear God on something that might make them stand alone with a specific word from God.

It is OK to start at this level. This entry level is meant to have boundaries yet allow us room to learn to step out. These boundaries mean there is little risk involved and little accountability required for what we hear. The boundaries at the bottom of the mountain provide a safe environment where we can learn to hear God's voice under the care of a good pastor like Moses.

2. Visions, dreams, and leadership level

> Then Moses went up, also Aaron, Nadab, and Abihu, and seventy of the elders of Israel, and they saw the God of Israel. And there was under His feet as it were a paved work of sapphire stone, and it was like the very heavens in its clarity. But on the nobles of the children of Israel He did not lay His hand. So they saw God, and they ate and drank.
>
> —EXODUS 24:9–11

This is a higher level, where it isn't just prophetic secrets of exhortation, edification, and comfort. This level may include visions and dreams that give guidance for specific situations. A person is ready to rise to this level when that person's leadership has proven fruit of service and the leader is positioned to lead others. As a result, God is able to reveal secrets on a deeper level because of the leader's ability to influence others.

However, visions and dreams and supernatural experiences from God are not restricted just to those in leadership. The more we grow in our character and submit our giftings to the Lord and to a good church and pastor, the higher we can ascend in God. Samuel was one of the greatest prophets ever, but he had to submit his giftings to the mentoring and training of Eli the priest.

The great apostle Paul was a prophet who used his gift faithfully in the church of Antioch before being sent out for a broader ministry by the Holy Ghost in Acts 13. The important thing to remember is that deeper secrets from God require a proven lifestyle and submission of ministry.

3. Spiritual mentoring level

> So Moses arose with his assistant Joshua, and Moses went up to the mountain of God.
>
> —EXODUS 24:13

This third level is where you have started at the beginning and are learning to hear the secrets of God. In addition, you have served faithfully under good leadership. Now God begins to groom you with some intensive hands-on training. It is like graduating from being a doctor to one who is a specialist in some field of medicine. You cannot become a specialist by watching TV or taking an Internet course. You must sit under the personal instruction and training of someone else—a mentor dedicated to giving you personal training.

Just so, this level of spiritual mentoring requires a personal relationship with mentors in your life who can teach you and guide you for that call. Like with Joshua, who was mentored by Moses, this requires intensive development to prepare you to minister on a regular ministry basis. Often this is related to a specific ministry calling.

4. Face-to-face level

> Then Moses went up into the mountain, and a cloud covered the mountain.
> —EXODUS 24:15

> So the LORD spoke to Moses face to face, as a man speaks to his friend.
> —EXODUS 33:11

This is the level where God speaks very specific things to you face-to-face, things that could literally change the course of history on a large scale. Notice that Moses, the leader, went to this place alone. Now, I am not saying that we cannot have a face-to-face experience with God as a Christian without experiencing all these levels. We can always get alone with God and hear our Father's heart! However, I believe a face-to-face relationship as a Christian is much different from a face-to-face impartation of secrets that guide and direct the lives of others, especially when it comes to large groups of people.

It is like the time when John the Beloved leaned on the breast of

Jesus, listening to His heart! Jesus was John's ministry mentor. But Jesus was also the heartbeat of God that John heard very closely, specifically, and deeply. Could it be that John's experience of leaning on the breast of Jesus helped to prepare him to receive the revelation on the island of Patmos? It requires practice, mentoring, and training to hear for others at this level of specific, directive prophecy, but it also means that we know how to encounter God face-to-face—and are skilled at it.

Some of the secrets from God that you hear at this level may be sounds you don't necessarily want to hear. You may have to stand alone and risk appearing foolish. In some cases, you may face vehement persecution. Remember that the people often wanted to stone Moses for speaking specific things from God. Not everyone is called to this level or can handle it. However, each of us has received a calling from God, and if we are called to this level, we must stay where we are called, and we will be blessed as a result.

If you are called to this level of hearing from God, spend intimate time with God. If, like Moses, you are called to hear secrets on a leadership level, others will confirm it, and it will become evident to you and others around you.

I encourage you to make a decision to come up to a new level of hunger and dedication for God's secrets. We live in a day when we need all the secrets of the Lord—whether general or specific, and we should not despise or treat any of them as insignificant. The world needs to know what God is saying, whether it sounds like thunder or is as clear as a bell.

Prepare yourself to receive God's heavenly throne-room secrets in your life. No matter how God chooses to share His secrets with you, believe that you are able to receive His secrets for whatever He wants to accomplish through you. If you are willing, you can learn to hear the secrets God wants to give you, and it will always produce a blessing.

TWO

THE REVEALER OF
SECRETS HAS COME

But there is a God in heaven who reveals secrets.
                                                  –Daniel 2:28

T HE REVEALER OF SECRETS HAS SURELY COME, AND HE IS revealing countless secrets to us today. You should be encouraged to know that God cares enough to speak to you. How discouraging it would be if the only voice we ever heard was all the negative reports, stories, and events we see on television. Take the time to learn how to hear the secrets of the Lord. If you are willing, the Lord will use many ways to teach—even, sometimes, unusual methods!

A few years before I married, I began asking the Lord to hear specific secrets and words from Him. One late evening in October, just before Halloween, I had just gotten off work. I was supposed to meet up with my roommate to go street witnessing. Before we went, I decided to take time to pray and ask God for specific direction about our time of witnessing. I didn't pray any fancy prayers, just a simple one asking the Holy Spirit to direct us where to go and with whom to speak. What happened later that night would forever change my life, and it still causes me to laugh at God's wonderful sense of humor!

THE TWO DEVILS ON E STREET

During that prayer, I kept hearing some odd words coming into my spirit. At first they came suddenly, but they stayed with me. The Lord had to repeat the words to me several times before I caught on to the reality that God was talking to me. This is what I kept hearing: "Go to E Street across the river. There is a party with loud music. Go witness to them!"

I decided to act on what I kept hearing and told my roommate what I heard. He looked at me, kind of laughing, and said, "OK, let's go!" He was always one for bold radical things, so he was more than game to go.

With just this one directive, we headed out, not knowing what to expect when we arrived. We drove across the river and headed toward E Street. We drove up and down the block for about forty-five minutes and did not hear any loud music or party or see any cars lined up on the street that would indicate a party. The street looked completely opposite of what I heard. "How could this be?" I thought. I asked my roommate, who was driving, if he was sure we were on the right street.

He said, "Sure, man. See the sign? We are on F Street like you said!"

"What!" I said. "I told you to go to E Street, not F Street."

So there we were on the wrong road, looking for the word of the Lord to come to pass. I guess I would rather be out there on the wrong road trying to follow the secret I heard than doing nothing at all! This is where some often find themselves—afraid to try because they might be making a mistake.

After renavigating our position, we arrived on E Street, and sure enough, we found exactly what the Lord had said. Except there was one problem—God never told us what to do next! I said, "Uh, God? I see the cars and hear the music and the party, but You never told us what to do next."

Doesn't that sound familiar? You hear what you believe is the Lord, but He doesn't exactly tell you what to do about it. With God, I have learned to act on what He says, and the rest of the information usually will come.

There we stood, staring at the house and listening to the music blaring into the street. "So, Lord, if we are going to witness to these people, how are we going to get into the house? I mean, it's not like we were invited to the party, so we can't just knock on the door and ask to join them."

Then, just minutes later, two guys dressed like devils—literally—came out of the house. Their costumes were red, complete with long tails and horns. Remember, it was Halloween, but these two looked more like they were dressed for a comedy show than a Halloween party. We sat there laughing hysterically at their ridiculous outfits. Immediately it became clear that they were intoxicated. Before tripping back toward the house, these two characters decided to use the side of the house for a quick pit stop!

Right then we made our move! We walked quickly up to them standing there. Just as we approached, one of them looked up to see us and blurted out in slurred speech, "Look! It's two angels!"

"Wow!" said the other, trying to point at us without falling over, still holding his cup of brew. "Angels!"

The next thing we knew, we were being escorted into the party by two drunken devils to witness for Jesus! A little nervous, we came inside feeling a bit out of place, but just then, one of the *devils* boldly announced that some angels wanted to talk to them. That devil was prophesying and didn't even know it! I often thought I should have told them I was Gabriel.

I looked around the room, and before I could stop my mouth, I heard myself telling them to stop the music and the TV because I had something to say—a pretty bold thing to say when you are not a real angel.

With that, a very muscular, college-aged man came from the crowd and asked us just what we thought we were doing. All the while, our devil friends kept insisting to everyone that we were angels. They told everyone that they needed to listen because we were sent from heaven. Of course, the muscular man, also the owner of the home, didn't think we were angels at all and didn't want us there.

To our shock, however, and to calm his two friends who were convinced we *were* angels, he let us talk briefly. For a few moments we shared the love of Jesus and witnessed to the entire group. Now, no one made an up-front commitment to the Lord that night that we were aware of, but we sure gave the gospel to them. I believe we will one day see the fruit of that event, but it wouldn't have happened had I not stepped out in my effort to hear from the Lord.

COMMON PEOPLE WITH UNCOMMON SECRETS

We can see from this story just how one word from God can truly make a difference in our lives and the lives of others. I realize this story may seem bold for some, and we don't have to always do radical things like this to hear specific secrets from God. What I want you to see is that God does speak specifics for the purpose of blessing people. You don't have to feel perfectly qualified to hear from God, either. In fact, God loves using people who are humble and the least likely candidates by human standards.

Look at some of the disciples the Lord chose. At first they were very raw material. Yet, they turned the world upside down and learned the treasure of listening to the Lord and obeying Him. In reality, the secret God gave me about E Street was no different from the word Ananias received in Acts 9:10–11. This disciple was just a common man. He is only mentioned briefly. He wasn't a great apostle or even referred to as a prophet, but God gave him one secret that helped form the early church.

Look at this common man with an uncommon secret:

> Now there was a certain disciple at Damascus named Ananias; and to him the Lord said in a vision, "Ananias." And he said, "Here I am, Lord." So the Lord said to him, "Arise and go to the street called Straight, and inquire at the house of Judas for one called Saul of Tarsus, for behold, he is praying. And in a vision he has seen a man named Ananias coming in and putting his hand on him, so that he might receive his sight."
>
> —ACTS 9:10-12

All Ananias said was, "I am here, Lord." That's right, he was a disciple, a simple Christian who loved the Lord, and all he did was make himself available. His willingness to hear the Lord helped steer the apostle Paul on his journey toward ministry. Thank God that this everyday disciple was listening to God! Here's the key: he made himself available for the Lord's use. What if he had been afraid of missing it? What if he just assumed that God would choose someone else to speak to?

The way to begin hearing is to first become available. Then start expecting God to speak to you. If you will, He will do so regardless of your level of boldness or experience. Perhaps the reason we don't hear from the Revealer of secrets is because we aren't expecting to hear anything. Hearing Him begins with listening for Him until His voice comes. Don't just try to hear at first and then walk away and tell yourself, "Well, I guess God just doesn't speak to me." No! If you will expect to hear, you will find that God is just waiting to talk. He longs to say things to you this way. He wants to discuss your future and the events still to come, but you have to believe He will talk to you about them. No, not someone else all the time, but you.

In Daniel 2:29, we see how God revealed His secrets to the king: "As for you, O king, thoughts came to your mind while on your bed, about what would come to pass after this; and He who reveals secrets has made known to you what will be." Some believers think God is withholding secrets from them for some strange divine reason. That's what religion has often led us to believe. So instead of going to God to find answers, people go to psychics and read horoscopes to find their answers.

Many Christians find themselves guessing about what God might be saying. Sure, there are things God will hide from you because He knows you aren't ready to handle them, but in the middle of that, there will be plenty of things He does have to say about your situation or someone else's situation.

God has many thoughts about you and the people with whom you are involved. He asserts: "For I know the thoughts that I think toward you, says the LORD, thoughts of peace and not of evil, to give you a future and a hope" (Jeremiah 29:11). The Lord has many things to reveal. He just needs those who will make themselves available and step out.

Sure, there may be times when it feels like foolishness to step out and test what you are hearing. But, as in my experience on E Street, what did it hurt to drive over there? Praise God that we did! It may not always feel comfortable when God reveals something, but then again, the Lord never said it would.

If you still doubt that God can speak specifically to you, let me give you some further scriptures that reiterate this point. God has a lot of secrets to tell because the Revealer of secrets has come:

> He reveals deep and secret things; He knows what is in the darkness.
> —DANIEL 2:22

> There is a God in heaven who reveals secrets.
> —DANIEL 2:28

> He who reveals secrets has made known to you what will be.
> —DANIEL 2:29

The great God has made known to the king what will
come to pass after this.
—DANIEL 2:45

Surely the Lord GOD does nothing, unless He reveals
His secret to His servants the prophets.
—AMOS 3:7

He...declares to man what his thought is.
—AMOS 4:13

The secret of the LORD is with those who fear Him.
—PSALM 25:14

His secret counsel is with the upright.
—PROVERBS 3:32

My sheep hear My voice, and I know them, and they
follow Me.
—JOHN 10:27

This does not sound like a God who isn't talking. If we want to hear
Him, we have to listen and believe it. Then, get ready—the secrets will
come your way!

WHERE ARE YOU?

In the beginning, Adam had the privilege of hearing God's voice. He
walked with God in the cool of the day and had conversations with the
Revealer of secrets—God Himself. After Adam sinned, his communication with God was interrupted. In fact, Adam not only quit talking
with the Lord, but he also hid from Him (Genesis 3:8–9). Why do you
suppose he hid? Sure, the shame of his sin was the main reason. But I
also think that Adam began to feel God no longer wanted to talk to him
as He once had done.

However, God still looked for Adam. He asked, "Where are you?" Adam could no longer be found in the same place, ready to communicate with the Lord, because of his failure.

You may think that you are just like Adam and have done so many things wrong that you can no longer hear from the Lord anymore. That is not exactly true. Sin can disrupt your relationship with God and make His voice difficult to hear. But God does not quit attempting to speak to you just because you make a mistake.

Notice that the Lord still called out to Adam. He wanted to speak to Adam even after he sinned. Furthermore, consider the example of Adam's son Cain. He had just murdered his brother Abel, and yet the Lord came to talk to him about it. God will still reach out to speak to you even when you blow it. The most important thing to remember is to respond to Him and repent of any wrongdoing. This will bring you back into right relationship. Habitual sin and refusal to repent or live right will eventually distance you from God. However, don't just assume that because you make one mistake or have areas in your life where you are working to correct things that God quits talking and has given up on you. Keep running to God, and listen to His voice.

If you have made mistakes, backslidden, or failed miserably, get it right, and get back to God. The more you seek to please Him and walk in His ways, the more He will speak to you. Pick yourself up, and keep your heart soft and clean. Then, as you pursue a righteous lifestyle, position yourself to hear. Adam made a mistake by not positioning himself to hear the Lord. Instead, he ran away and hid. If you stay connected to God on a daily basis, He will not have to continually ask, "Where are you?" as He did with Adam.

I am reminded of a time when my wife, Brenda, and I were ministering overseas at a conference. In the hotel, our phone rang constantly. Each time we answered, the person on the other line would be speaking something in a foreign language. This went on all night without any peace and quiet. Every time I picked up the phone to answer it, someone was speaking in a foreign language I didn't understand. I found out later from our interpreter that the calls were from prostitutes. The interpreter told us they get business by calling hotel rooms. So I decided that the next night when the calls came, I would be ready with a confrontation. Since I couldn't speak a single word in their language, all I could do was pray in the Spirit on the phone. The phone rang, and I prayed in tongues loudly in the ear of the person calling and then slammed the phone down. I told my wife how anointed I felt when I prayed while on the phone.

I am not kidding when I say that we had absolute silence for days, while the rest of our team complained about these calls. I felt such a strong anointing for what I had done to stop my calls that I told the others about it and suggested they do the same! However, when we prepared to check out of the hotel, I was stunned to discover that my moment of spiritual power had a simple explanation—when I slammed the phone down, I knocked it off the hook! There had been no connection—no power—after that at all. I'm sure you can understand when I tell you that my wife wasn't thrilled when she realized that our kids had not been able to call our room for days!

Do you know that this is exactly what we do with our walk with God? In our moments of discouragement and frustration, we disconnect without realizing it. We are no longer in position to receive His voice. So He looks at us and asks, "Where are you?" Like the phone in that hotel room, we are the ones who are disconnected when God is quiet and doesn't seem to be talking. Out of frustration, anger, and other reasons, we cut off His voice even though He wants to speak.

We need constant fellowship and a continual connection with God in order to hear Him and position ourselves for heaven's visitation. We get in position through daily prayer and Bible reading and by living right and keeping the conversation going with Him throughout the day. He should not have to ask, "Where are you?" If we want to hear His secrets, we have to be in position to hear.

Have you ever wondered how the apostle Paul could know and write about the events happening in the churches while he was in prison? There were people who visited him while he was in prison, but I believe he also knew what God was doing because the spirit of wisdom and revelation was in communication with him daily. He promised this to us in Ephesians 1:15–17:

> Therefore I also, after I heard of your faith in the Lord Jesus and your love for all the saints, do not cease to give thanks for you, making mention of you in my prayers: that the God of our Lord Jesus Christ, the Father of glory, may give to you the spirit of wisdom and revelation in the knowledge of Him.

The Holy Spirit gave wisdom and revelation to Paul because he was constantly connected to God, even in the midst of his horrible situation in jail.

There is another important clue as to how Paul stayed connected to God in 1 Corinthians 14:18: "I thank my God I speak with tongues more than you all." This is a key principle that will also work in your life no matter what you are facing or how terrible things are. Paul made a habit of praying in tongues. I am convinced that he must have prayed in tongues while in prison too!

When we are filled, or baptized, in the Holy Spirit, we receive a well of power on the inside. Jesus said, "'He who believes in Me, as the Scripture has said, out of his heart will flow rivers of living water.' But this He spoke concerning the Spirit, whom those believing in Him would receive; for the Holy Spirit was not yet given, because Jesus was not yet glorified" (John 7:38–39). Each time Paul prayed in tongues in prison, he tapped into the river of living water or power inside him.

One of the ways that we tap into this well filled with power and gain access to heaven's secrets is through praying in the Spirit. There is little doubt that Paul tapped into heavenly secrets from his prison cell just by praying in the Spirit. During those times of praying in tongues, I am certain many things were revealed to him about the situations around him and those in the churches.

We can see this principle further in the first miracle of Jesus. In John 2, Jesus turned the water into wine after telling the servants to fill six water pots full of water. Notice the servants filled the six pots at Jesus's instruction, and then He told them to do something else. He told them to draw out some of the water (John 2:8). When they did, they discovered it had turned into new wine!

Isn't that what happened on the Day of Pentecost? Those gathered in the Upper Room were filled with the water of the Spirit, but when they drew it out by praying in tongues, out came the new wine! In fact, many standing by thought they were drunk.

Ephesians 6:18 tells us to be filled with the Spirit. Why? Because in the Spirit is where the secrets of heaven are found. One of Paul's instructions to the church was: "Therefore let him who speaks in a tongue pray that he may interpret" (1 Corinthians 14:13). We are to pray that we may interpret our tongues. This doesn't mean that every time you pray in tongues you need an interpretation. You need an interpretation when you are in a public service where God is giving a message in tongues for the purpose of the congregation. This is not the same as praying in tongues for prayer and fellowship directly to God. Could it be possible that as Paul prayed in tongues from his prison cell, he also had times when he interpreted those tongues? In such a way he was drawing from the well of the Spirit within.

You too can draw the secrets of heaven from within in your spirit, and this enables you to stay connected to the Lord. The more you pray in the Spirit, the more you have access to the whispers of heaven's secrets. You are connected to heaven, and throne-room revelation is made available to you!

I have noticed in my own life and ministry that the more I pray in the Spirit, the more I hear from the Lord. In fact, the more I pray in the Spirit and draw out of my inner man, the more specific the word of the Lord becomes. I like to pray in the Spirit wherever I can. Each day I quietly pray under my breath as I walk throughout the day, staying connected to heaven.

Years before I entered the ministry, there was one day when I received a throne-room secret while working in a service station. I had been praying in the Spirit under my breath that day, not making a scene with it and still continuing to work. After all, I was being paid and was expected to work. As I stocked the shelves, a customer pulled up to fill his car with gas from the self-serve island. As the customer came in to pay for the gasoline and I began to ring up the sale, I heard the Holy Spirit whisper in my heart.

"Tell him that I love him and that he once served Me but is now running from Me. Let him know that I know he is hurting because his relative just died. I know that he is going through a tough time." It was incredible! Before I had time to think, I repeated to the customer what I had just heard.

Within seconds, the customer's eyes filled with tears, and he said, "What you're saying is correct."

My boss even suggested that I step out of the room and pray with the man! Thank God, that person rededicated his life to the Lord that day. I wasn't planning on ministering to this stranger or sharing a prophetic secret, but God was able to arrange it because I was drawing from the well inside me all day.

I like what the great man of God Smith Wigglesworth said when asked how long he prayed. People wanted to know because of the profound miracles that he had in his ministry. So he replied to the question, "I don't often spend more than half an hour in prayer at one time, but I never go more than half an hour without praying."[1]

We can follow his example. We can maintain a lifestyle of prayer and watch the reward of God communicating to and through us all day. Perhaps you have not been filled with the Holy Spirit or spoken in tongues yet. I want to invite you to go to the back of this book for further instruction. If you have been baptized in the Holy Spirit and speak in other tongues, I want to encourage you to increase the amount of time that you pray in your heavenly language. You will see the difference if you will stay with it.

Follow the apostle Paul's encouragement to pray to be able to interpret what you say when speaking in the Spirit. One of the best ways to do this is by writing down the thoughts and words that you hear as you speak in the Spirit. Another way is to start speaking in your native language the words you hear in your heart as you pray in the Spirit. You may be surprised at the good things that come out! The most important thing is to stay connected, fill yourself up with your heavenly language, and be ready for the whispers of God to come to you.

PROGRESSING IN THE SECRET THINGS

I have found that learning to receive the whispers of God is a progressive experience. We know Scripture tells us we go from glory to glory and faith to faith. This is the way it is in the prophetic. We step out and try little by little until a genuine flow of God's secrets begins coming into our lives. Each of us must progress in hearing the secrets of God. Romans 12:3, 6, tells us: "God has dealt to each one a measure of faith.... Having then gifts differing according to the grace that is given to us, let us use them: if prophecy, let us prophesy in proportion to our faith." Notice that we are instructed to prophesy according to the measure of faith we have been given. Each of us has a measure of faith to speak the secrets of God. It is up to us to develop that faith and cause it to mature and grow in our lives.

Look at the example of Joseph. He began with a dream he received for *himself*, and then, later in his life, he started interpreting dreams for *others*. The Lord had truly given this young man a gift that would later unfold into greater depths and responsibilities. Joseph became the right-hand man for Pharaoh—with responsibilities over all of Egypt. In

Genesis 41:46, we learn, "Pharaoh called Joseph's name Zaphnathpaa-neah." This is significant and shows that Pharaoh recognized Joseph's ability to interpret dreams, because in the Coptic, that name signifies "a revealer of secrets, or the man to whom secrets are revealed."[2]

Notice how Joseph progressed when it came to hearing heavenly secrets:

- He first received a dream for himself of his future (Genesis 37).

- He then began to interpret dreams for others by minis-tering to the baker and the butler while he was in prison (Genesis 40).

- Finally, he progressed into prophetic abilities that eventu-ally brought him before the pharaoh himself (Genesis 41).

Realize that at first you might get one little phrase or picture—or not hear, see, or sense anything at all. The key is let it build in your life as you step out in faith. I remember that before I learned to hear from God, I had dreams but often didn't know what they meant. It was later I realized that God was speaking to me through dreams. Sometimes, learning to hear from God is as simple as the Lord putting a name of a person in your heart, maybe someone you haven't thought about for some time. God may cause you to feel that you should call someone. These seemingly insignificant ways can develop your progression of learning to receive secrets from God.

When you do recognize that you are beginning to hear things from God, find someone you can trust to bounce things off. A good church, pastor, and other mature believers are so helpful and needed. Ask them their thoughts on things you are hearing and what you should consider doing with the things you hear.

When I was a very young Christian, a girl I knew was in a very serious car accident that left her in a coma. Although I prayed about this in my time with the Lord, I never felt anything specific. Then one night I had a dream that this young girl would wake up out of her coma before Easter Sunday. I woke up thinking, "Did I just dream that?" At that time, I wasn't attending a good church and did not know a believer who could give me some feedback, so I shared this with a few unsaved people who laughed at me and persecuted me, much as people did to Joseph. They told me that God didn't speak today and my dream was not from the Lord. It is important to be careful whom you share your dreams with. You don't have to share everything you believe you have heard from God.

But the dream was from God, and the girl did wake up just before Easter! However, even that didn't convince these people that God speaks today. They believed it was just a coincidence, and all my sharing did was create conflict.

We have to use caution about the people we share with, because sharing may make matters worse for you, even if your hearing was accurate. Isn't that what happened to Joseph? He shared his dream with his brothers and got sold into slavery. Not everyone is ready to hear or handle what you are hearing. Obviously, Joseph's brothers couldn't handle it! Perhaps things would have happened differently for Joseph had he not shared it with them.

This is why developing your gift under a good pastor who believes and supports the things of the Holy Spirit is necessary and vital for progressing in the things of God. He or she can help you learn the proper prophetic manners and protocol that will bring longevity of your gift.

Your progression in hearing God's secrets will also require that you develop wisdom. Once you hear from God, you must know what to do with the thing you have heard. At times, God wants you to share with others what He has told you. At other times, you should be silent until the right place and the right time for sharing.

Even though you may have a specific word to share, the setting may not be right for sharing it. When I am ministering with a word from God publicly, I have had to learn to use wisdom and manners with the person to whom I am ministering. Never expose, embarrass, or open another person's heart in public, whether you are dealing with a sin issue or not. For the most part, people's business should remain personal.

When I am ministering in public, if God is asking me to share something corrective or very personal with one person, I usually turn the microphone off and minister to that person privately. In some cases I wait until after the service. How would you like everyone knowing your business? As I have grown in God, I have come to understand that public rebuke should be reserved for the most severe cases or as a last resort—as when it calls someone to salvation or spiritual restoration. We must be honorable when sharing the word of the Lord.

The more you progress in hearing and receiving sensitive information from the Lord, the more wisdom you need to know how to respond to and handle what you receive.

I remember a time when I should have used better wisdom while ministering to a man in a service where I was speaking. I told this man that he was called to be a pastor, and I even strongly implied that God wanted him to be added to the pastoral staff of that church. The pastor later confirmed that, indeed, he was considering the man for the church staff. However, he did not yet have peace about the timing of this transition and was waiting to hear more specifically from God.

It was a right word that I heard, but it wasn't wise to share it publicly. As a result of this word from God, the man became impatient and fell into horrible pride. He tried to usurp authority over the senior pastor in order to get placed on staff. I should have shared this word privately with the pastor first. My decision to share publicly put this senior pastor in a very difficult position in front of his church, especially when everyone witnessed the man's bad behavior later. He eventually left the church offended, never fulfilling what the Lord intended.

Another example of prophesying unwisely happened in a meeting at a local church where a visiting minister prophesied to the pastor and his wife that they were to have another baby. However, this couple already had children and did not feel led to have any more, even after this event and more personal prayer.

For a long time, the people in the church nagged this couple about fulfilling the prophecy with another child, giving a subtle message that either the pastoral couple was ignoring the word or the messenger missed it. It would have been far better for the minister to share this personal type of information privately and avoid putting these pastors on public display, opening their private life for all to judge and offer input.

Some words from God are meant to be shared privately. It is important to handle prophetic gifts with wisdom and clarity. The prophetic has been so misunderstood and attacked today. By using wisdom, manners, and good protocol, we can preserve this great gift.

We can learn how to progress in hearing the secrets of God with both accuracy and wisdom from the life of one of my favorite characters in the Bible, Moses. When he heard the voice of God speaking to him from a burning bush, he was surprised! At that point, he was in the beginning stages of hearing God. Just like us, Moses had to progress in hearing God's secrets and handling them properly. We can see this progression in the following examples:

- *He spent time as a shepherd.* He had to develop a true heart for the sheep. This speaks of developing a heart for God's people. He had to learn things from both perspectives—respect for the shepherd and respect for the sheep.

- *He served his father-in-law.* This is likened to serving in the local church. We learn to serve and work for others in our heavenly Father's sheepfold. The apostle Paul served in the local church at Antioch before he was commissioned as an apostle (Acts 13:1).

- *He was hidden in the backside of the desert.* He was not seen or visible in any form of public ministry during these forty long years. He wasn't in a position of royalty or in the spotlight, as he would be later in Egypt. His pride was being crucified, and greatness was being developed in him.

- *He was told to take off his shoes.* This was a sign of respect to a superior. He was learning the importance of submission and honoring proper authority. Today many people are never raised up properly because they fail to learn proper spiritual authority and proper protocol for the prophetic.

No More Excuses

Of course, even the most skilled hearers of God's secrets will find times when they want to make excuses for why they are not qualified for certain tasks that the Lord gives them. Some people just want to let someone else hear God's secrets and don't want to do what it takes to progress and grow in the secrets of God. Moses makes a great example for us to learn from in this area. Not only was it of great necessity for Moses to be properly prepared, trained, and equipped to carry the precious word of the Lord, but he also needed to be delivered from all the reasons he voiced in resistance. Listed below are excuses that Moses gave to the Lord for why he didn't feel he could deliver God's secrets. They sound like the same excuses we give the Lord for why we can't hear Him or why we fail to progress in becoming the properly qualified vessels to bring His secrets to the world.

"Who am I?"—Exodus 3:11

At one time, Moses lived in the house of Pharaoh as a member of the ruling family in Egypt. Now he had become a shepherd. He wasn't feeling qualified or confident in himself. This is exactly how we may feel when we try to hear from God. We think we aren't qualified. A low self-esteem, fear of rejection, and lack of confidence can hinder us in stepping out in the secrets of God.

What's the answer to the "who am I" mentality? God answered Moses the same way He is answering all of us: "I will certainly be with you" (Exodus 3:12). In other words, God will help you, and you can do it! But you will have to quit implying that you aren't qualified, because God with you qualifies you automatically! With God's help, you can speak His secrets. You just need to rely upon God and be willing to learn. "I can do all things through Christ who strengthens me" (Philippians 4:13).

"What shall I say?"—Exodus 3:13

Maybe Moses wasn't as concerned about what he would say as he was about how others would perceive his words. Perhaps he was fearful of his reputation and didn't want his words to appear foolish. He might have been afraid he couldn't answer the questions of his adversaries. His concern about his reputation caused him to let fear talk him out of being used by God.

The apostle Paul told his spiritual son, Timothy, not to be afraid of the gifts God had given to him, and he told him to *stir up* his gift. "Therefore I remind you to stir up the gift of God which is in you through the laying on of my hands. For God has not given us a spirit of fear, but of power and of love and of a sound mind" (2 Timothy 1:6–7). God has given us the ability to hear His voice and share His secrets, and we must not let fear talk us out of it. We must stir it up!

It's kind of like making Kool-Aid. If you put sugar and Kool-Aid in the pitcher of water but don't stir it, the ingredients will just settle to the bottom and will not taste right. In the same way, we stir up our gift by praying in the Spirit and stepping out to prophesy the word of the Lord. Look at God's response to Moses in Exodus 3:14: "And He said, 'Thus you shall say....'" God was saying, "You have nothing to be afraid of. I am telling you to step out, Moses, and say it!" We should be encouraged to step out and say it and not be fearful of our reputation.

"Suppose they will not believe?"–Exodus 4:1

Moses was saying, "God, what if they won't listen?" I have felt that way before. You step out with what you believe to be God, but somebody tries to discourage you and resist you. However, in Exodus 4, God proved three times that He was with Moses, which served as a sign to his hearers:

1. *The rod* (verses 2–5)—Moses's rod turned into a serpent and swallowed the serpent of the enemy. This speaks of the authority we have over the devil as believers in Jesus Christ. We have supernatural power—God's power—over the enemy. When you speak with God's secrets, He will back you with power while you speak.

2. *Moses's hand turned leprous* (verses 6–8)—Leprosy speaks of sin or the sinner. We come with secrets that speak specifically to the heart of the sinner. They will be tailor-made as a sign that will open their hearts to convert them. When their hearts are changed, it will serve as proof of God's power on you.

3. *The water turned to blood* (verse 9)—The water and blood go together (1 John 5:8). Moses was instructed to take water out of the river and pour it on dry ground, where it would be changed to blood. This part speaks of the word of God inside of us. It may be either the water of the written Word of God (Ephesians 5:26) or the *rhema*, which is God's spoken word given to us by His Spirit. We have the authority to take this word from the river of the Spirit because of our blood covenant in Jesus Christ. People will receive proof

of your ministry because you come with the truth of the gospel, which is the power of God for salvation.

"I am slow of speech and slow of tongue!"—Exodus 4:10

Moses, like us, started looking at his faults and inadequacies. We say things like "I am not good at this," "God doesn't speak to me like that," and "I don't know how to hear from Him, and besides, I am not the best speaker anyway." I remember the first time I had to speak publicly. I was in eighth grade doing a speech. Everyone could see the huge sweat stains on my shirt clear down to my waist. I was shaking as I read my speech. A teacher even told me in a joking way (I don't think she meant it to be hurtful) that I wasn't a great speaker, and she suggested that I should not pursue public speaking! Today God, with His sense of humor, has called my wife and me to stand before crowds of thousands and preach! I could have said, "Forget it, I am not good at that." God just wants an available and willing voice! Can He use you?

"Please send...whomever else You may send!"—Exodus 4:13

Now the truth really comes out with Moses! This was the real reason, above all the previous excuses. He just didn't want to do it! He wanted someone else to do it. "Let it be someone else's responsibility—just don't let it be mine!" We think someone else can do it better, or perhaps we just don't want to be troubled with it. Face it—it takes a lot of work to grow in something you haven't done before. We have to decide that we are willing to progress in God's secrets and grow in whatever way He wants to use us.

Maybe you feel like these excuses pretty much describe where you are. Perhaps you feel like it's a tall order to grow in the secrets of God and to mature to the point that God can trust you with the responsibility of His secrets. Maybe you would much rather have someone else speak the word of the Lord to you. Don't let that be the case. Let the greatness inside of you come out, and determine that hearing God's secrets is not a difficult thing. Sure, it is progressive, but each time you do it, it will get easier. You will be surprised at the accurate things you hear from God. Keep your spirit full of His Word, and pray in the Spirit often. Suddenly, you will find yourself tapping into a well of God's secrets for you and for others. Yes, you have been born to learn to hear God's secrets.

THREE

REQUIREMENTS FOR
LAST-DAY PROPHECY

God, who at various times and in various ways
spoke in time past to the fathers by the prophets,
has in these last days spoken to us by His Son.

—Hebrews 1:1–2

"GO TELL THE COUPLE AT THE TABLE ACROSS THE RESTAURANT that I want to speak to them."

"What?" I thought as I continued eating, simply enjoying a date with my wife. I looked up to see if my wife noticed my stirring. I had identified the couple I believed the Lord was speaking to me about, but I was not about to obey. I reasoned in my mind two important factors: first, I was on a date with my wife, so I was not in a mind to minister to anyone, and, second, these people were strangers.

I have found that ministering in the prophetic is like a radio. Sometimes you enjoy the sound, other times you need to fine-tune it, and then there are times when you need to turn it off—especially when you are on a date with your wife! I am not saying to turn the Lord's voice off; I am saying there are times we need to turn off "prophetic mode."

In this case, I was not in prophetic mode. Additionally, these people also appeared to be on a date, so I reasoned they didn't want to be bothered.

So I continued eating, but the more I ate, the more uncomfortable I got. This whisper in my heart would not leave. I had hoped that the couple would leave, then surely I wouldn't have to talk to them, and, better yet, maybe I wasn't hearing God after all! My wife and I were almost ready to leave, and there that couple sat, still talking. Should I ignore this secret I heard or go for it? My wife and I approached these strangers sitting at a table.

Since they didn't know me, and it is not my nature to approach people I don't know with this type of prophetic word, I introduced myself and tried to be extra polite. Then I said very kindly, "I believe I heard the Lord tell me that the two of you were discussing whether or not to have children, and God wants me to tell you that He will provide, and it will be OK."

To my surprise, the couple at the table was more than hospitable. I believe they were open to us because we were polite, brief, and nonthreatening. We found out they were also Christians. Had they not been so welcoming, we would have cut it short and bid good-bye; however, they invited us to join them, and we were able to continue ministering to them. You see, it is important to watch someone's body language in a situation like this. If they seem distant and unresponsive, then that is an indication to politely end the conversation. This couple wanted to talk, and we even ended up helping them receive the baptism of the Holy Spirit outside the restaurant in their car! We were able to know them for years to follow, and they did have a child. God used that situation to touch their lives, but it may not have been accomplished had my wife and I not exemplified two things: a godly, orderly example of Jesus and proper manners and methods in how we ministered.

Again, I normally never would go up to someone I don't know and speak to them about their family planning, but this was one case when

I could not shake the word in my heart. When it's not in my plans to minister to anyone and the situation puts me outside of my comfort zone, I usually know it's the Lord! In cases when I do step out and minister to a perfect stranger, I always try first to connect with them through nonthreatening, basic conversation that may lead to me sharing what God might be saying.

JESUS SPEAKS THROUGH US

According to the scripture in Hebrews 1:1–2, *Jesus* is the One who speaks to the world today. How does He do that? Obviously, the answer is through us. However, we will only be able to speak effectively for Him when our lives are presented in godly order and our methods are biblical and proper. We have to learn God's methods so people will hear us. It requires flexibility and a willingness to take the focus off self. This is because God will ask you to do things that may not be comfortable for you or may not be your preferred method of ministry. He will ask you to do things that humble you and test your motives.

For example, when Jesus healed the blind, in one case He did it with laying on of His hands and His spoken word. In another case, when ministering to a blind man, He put saliva on the man's eyes. You had better know you are hearing from God when you start spitting on people!

All in all, different circumstances require different methods, and God's methods will require you to put your pride aside. Here are some questions you can ask yourself that will help you check your methods and decide if you are acting as a mature and proper spokesman for Jesus:

1. *Can the word wait, or is it needed right now?* Waiting on the word allows you time to search your heart, listen to God more intently, and make sure your motives, word, and timing are all correct. This way you can be sure it is actually Jesus who wants to say something—not you.

Sometimes you may even find the word from God doesn't need to be shared; God just wanted you to pray about it instead.

2. *How am I representing myself?* Be honest with yourself. Often when it comes to the prophetic, people get weird. They can't just act like normal human beings, and they scare people. They think prophesying gives them license to be dramatic, flakey, rude, and interruptive. Sometimes they even lose their gentleman or ladylike conduct. I would encourage you to take a second look at your social graces. Things like sloppy clothes, bad breath, and loud talking can turn people off to you. I can't say enough about that.

3. *What method does the Lord want to use?* Prophecy does not have to be shared in the typical "And the Lord would say to you..." method. Like the couple at the table, it can be through normal conversation. In other cases, it can be an offer to pray (and when I say pray, I mean just prayer, not prayer with the intent to prophesy). Do you know you can pray prophetically and never give a *textbook* prophecy? You can pray things like, "Lord, bless their house, and help them pay all their bills. Prosper them in their finances," instead of, "God says your finances will be blessed and your house paid for." See the difference? Find the method God wants you to use in every circumstance, and it will help you stay accurate and away from pride.

When people are set on their methods, they usually wind up doing more damage than good and hurt the prophetic things of God. It is important to be led of the Holy Spirit and to be open to hearing His voice, but the key to success is a focus on Jesus. Make sure He is the One they are hearing, because God wants to speak through His Son in the last days. Yes, He uses people, but Jesus is the One we want them to see and hear.

We must represent Jesus with humility and manners. There is a discipline and a maturing process to receiving the word of the Lord, holding on to it, and only sharing it at the right time and place.

I once shared a very specific word in a church service and was so excited to speak what I heard. After I shared the word and went back to my hotel room that night, I knew something was wrong. I could tell the Lord was not too happy with me. I sought God for an explanation to what I was feeling, and I realized that I had shared the right word at the wrong place and time.

Be assured that hearing from God is a learning process. There may be growing pains, but He is a good heavenly Father, and His Spirit is a great teacher! Allow the Lord time to teach you. Learn to speak when He wants you to speak—not just when you are in the mode of finding someplace to minister. Too many people feel the need to push their desire to speak a prophetic word. Relax. If God has something to say through you, He will provide the right platform at the right time. It is when I am not looking for it or don't want to share something that the word of the Lord often comes.

I want to encourage you to simply continue to be a normal daily example of Jesus's character and love. Stay tuned to the voice of the Holy Spirit, and let God open doors for you to minister for Him. Then when doors open for you, step out and test what you have been hearing. It's OK to try! I once heard a man say, "Jesus never rebuked His disciples for trying!"

It is always wise to start small and test what you are hearing. Start by asking a question or making small talk. This is exactly what Jesus did in John 4:16 with the woman at the well. He started by having a conversation about water with her *before* He told her to go call her husband. Without question, the Lord knew what her answer was going to be, but He used this kind method so as not to embarrass her.

Had Jesus been like many modern-day prophetic people, or even some ministers, He would have made sure He was addressing her before the church congregation so the powerful anointing could be witnessed. Then He would have told her plainly that she had been divorced five times and was now cohabitating with a man! I don't like it when people are embarrassed in front of others by a prophecy. I am convinced that some people do this kind of thing today because they want to draw attention to their prophetic anointing. Public embarrassment can make it much harder for people to hear and receive God's word, even if the word was accurate.

Jesus was a gentleman, and He spoke to her privately and in an indirect way that made it easier for her to receive. It wasn't until she was open about her life that He became more direct. He allowed her to open the door to the secrets before He shared them all. In fact, Jesus didn't even mention to her that He was a prophet. She was the one who said that (John 4:19). Jesus just reached out to her with manners and love, and it changed her life.

THE MAN AND HIS MESSAGE

We have to constantly remind ourselves that all prophecy comes through Jesus Christ. To speak prophetically, God uses prophetic people and prophets. To say we don't need prophets or prophecy today would be like saying we don't need pastors, teachers, or evangelists. Prophets are still part of the foundation of the church, and Jesus gave these gifts as His method for speaking His words. No, prophets are not those weird people you see on the news who lead cults, marry multiple wives, and wear funny robes! They are simply spokesmen and women who are ordained to share the things on the heart of Jesus for any given situation. Scripture tells us this:

- Apostles and prophets are set in the church to speak for the Lord (1 Corinthians 12:28).

- The Lord speaks through the fivefold ministry of apostles, prophets, evangelists, pastors, and teachers to equip the church (Ephesians 4:11).

- He speaks through Christians who hear His words (John 8:47).

- He speaks through Christians who hear and follow Him (John 10:27).

To do away with prophets and prophecy would be to do away with the importance of what prophecy does when ministered properly. According to 1 Corinthians 14:3, it is for the purpose of edification, exhortation, and comfort. Prophetic secrets are meant to be a blessing. Revelation 19:10 says, "The testimony of Jesus is the spirit of prophecy," and Revelation 1:2 says that John "bore witness to the word of God, and to the testimony of Jesus Christ, to all things that he saw." In simple terms, prophecy is whatever Jesus wants to say! When it places the focus on Jesus and what He wants to say (His Word), the result is that we are edified and comforted. You cannot have proper prophecy when Jesus and His majesty are not the focus. The testimony of Jesus (what He wants to say) and the spirit of prophecy go together. To receive the prophetic is to receive Jesus! To reject biblical prophesying and prophets is to reject Jesus.

It is sad that today some refuse the wonderful privilege of this grace gift, which can impact people's lives and testify of Jesus. They want to find every fault they can with either prophets or prophetic words.

For prophecy to be a blessing, however, the testimony or words of Jesus should be in every prophetic secret. It should testify of His Word and His character and bring honor and glory to Him, not to the one delivering the word. Whenever we prophesy, it must line up with the Bible and bring honor to the Lord Jesus! To exclude one or both is to separate two vital ingredients that make the prophetic word effective.

The testimony of Jesus and the spirit of prophecy are similar to the anointing oil. The anointing oil of the Old Testament required specific spices to make it correctly. You couldn't leave anything out. Prophecy and the testimony of Jesus are the same; you can't have one without the other. If you have the testimony of Jesus in your life, it means you have not only the words of Jesus, but you also have His character, His love, His methods, and all that represents Him. In turn, when you have the testimony of Jesus working all through your life, you can't help but be positioned to prophesy and give witness to Him!

In other words, the man and his message must be the same! Godly character, anointing, integrity, morals, honor, humility, and honesty, to name a few, must be who you are and part of the message you give. When you have these ingredients—like the ingredients of the anointing oil—people can better receive your message because the aroma will be right. It will smell and feel *right*.

But prophecy *without* the proper ingredients that give witness of Jesus is not honorable. The message and the one giving it must align correctly or it's not the testimony of Jesus Christ or the true spirit of prophecy.

Notice what it says in Ecclesiastes 10:1 (AMP): "Dead flies cause the ointment of the perfumer to putrefy [and] send forth a vile odor." Flies can be things like the flesh, religious mind-sets, religious mannerisms, manipulation, dishonesty, lack of order, bad manners, and rudeness, to name a few. When we try to mix these things with the power of God, it prevents people from receiving us and from being blessed by our message, because the ingredients have been defiled.

Take a look at what the prophet Ezekiel had to do to assure that he, the man, and his message would be the same: "He said to me, Son of man, eat what you find [in this book]; eat this scroll; then go and speak to the house of Israel" (Ezekiel 3:1, AMP). He had to *eat* the words given him on the scroll. The words of the scroll were his message or his *prophecy*. Literally, the words had to become a part of his person; they had to be the same.

We learn in the first chapter of Ezekiel that the word of the Lord and heavenly visions came in the thirtieth year of his life. Biblically, thirty was considered the age of maturity for a man. Joseph and King David were thirty years of age when they began to rule, and Jesus was thirty when His ministry began. For the prophet Ezekiel to give proper witness to his words, he had to live them and act as a mature man of God.

Years ago, before I was in the ministry, I visited a church service where I saw firsthand what happens when the man and his message are two different things. There were only about twenty people in attendance in this small church. The pastor told everyone he had a prophecy from the Lord, and it was that twenty people were to each give one hundred dollars in the offering. I knew it couldn't apply to me, because I was a single young man with only about ten dollars to my name. I certainly didn't have one hundred dollars!

The other nineteen people started running to the offering basket at the front, putting their offering envelope in it. I was the only one still sitting in my seat. The pastor then instructed everyone to close their eyes because one more person still had to obey the prophetic word. Everyone closed their eyes but me. I love to give and don't even mind being encouraged by the pastor to do so. Yet in my heart, I felt something was wrong.

The pastor prayed a loud prayer, asking God to fulfill His prophetic word and forgive the one in disobedience. I knew he was referring to me. I looked up and caught the pastor opening his eyes to see if I was listening and would obey. He quickly closed his eyes, knowing I had seen him. He shouted again, "There are twenty people who need to give one hundred dollars, and nineteen have obeyed the Lord. One still needs to give!" Can you believe it! I am telling you the truth; I got up and politely began to leave. This caused the pastor to yell all the more and to *prophesy* to me. I later found out from someone who knew that pastor that the other nineteen people in attendance were his close friends or relatives. Thank God I was smart enough to know this wasn't a prophecy from God. Those envelopes were probably empty!

I am all for God speaking a word that may invite the people to give a certain amount if done correctly with the testimony of Jesus behind it, but this was out of order. Sure, I have been in services where the Spirit of God moved greatly upon the people to give. However, this was not a correct word, and the spirit of the prophecy was false. It was given with compulsion, deceit, and manipulation. No testimony of Jesus's Word or character accompanied this pastor's prophecy!

This type of disorderly conduct only hinders the prophetic things of God, and it hurts the Lord's heart.

Even with all the flakiness and error in the prophetic, we need prophecy and God's secrets more than ever. Those who may abuse the precious word of the Lord should not stop us from seeking it! People are hungry for the real secrets of God because the world is so dark. In fact, in many ways we need to increase the prophetic word because so many places exist in a spiritual famine. Amos 8:11 says:

> "Behold, the days are coming," says the Lord GOD,
> "That I will send a famine on the land,
> Not a famine of bread,
> Nor a thirst for water,
> But of hearing the words of the LORD."

MAN'S CONDITION AND GOD'S SECRETS

Let's review the condition of the world and why we need to carry sharp and accurate words from God. It will make you hungry not only to deliver secrets of God but also to do what it takes to develop your methods and protocol in the prophetic.

Look at Genesis 1:2: "The earth was without form, and void; and darkness was on the face of the deep. And the Spirit of God was hovering over the face of the waters." This literal condition of the earth is also a prophetic picture of man's condition throughout history. The earth was without form, void and dark. This sounds a lot like the world today. People today are dark, without form, and void. What is their answer for their condition? They need prophetic secrets.

Notice the next thing that happened in Genesis 1: God spoke. He addressed the condition of the earth by saying something. He said, "Let there be light" (verse 3). God answered the condition with a prophecy that produced light. This is exactly what prophecy does; it sheds light or brings revelation to the desperate needs of mankind. It gives meaning to lives that have no meaning. They are void and without form or purpose. A good example of this can be found in the Book of Job.

> You will also declare a thing,
> And it will be established for you;
> So light will shine on your ways.
>
> —JOB 22:28

God's prophetic words will give light to your darkness. The prophetic decree of light from God can be compared to receiving revelation knowledge. When people receive a revelation, an idea, or an answer, they often say, "I saw the light," or "A light went off in my head." Prophecy or prophetic secrets, when spoken, shed light to those who are in darkness in one area or many.

First Corinthians 14:3 tells us that prophecy accomplishes three things: it edifies, exhorts, and comforts. Let's look at these in comparison to man's condition that we compared to the earth's condition at the beginning of Creation. Many people today are void, dark, and without form. I want to show you that prophecy is the answer for man's condition:

1. *Prophecy edifies those whose lives are without form.* Prophecy will strengthen you. When the whispers of God come through prophecy, it builds, or edifies, those whose

lives seem to be going nowhere. Suddenly a person who has no purpose gains new confidence to accomplish something positive. That is what it means to be edified; it strengthens you and gives you hope.

2. *Prophecy exhorts those who are in darkness.* Prophecy exhorts or gives direction. It gives you new ideas about what to do. It sheds light and new revelation about your situation. Exhortation is a directive, a game plan. It is easier to come out of darkness when you know what to do and where to go.

3. *Prophecy comforts those whose lives are void.* Prophecy comforts by filling your emptiness. A life that is void is a life with no meaning or fulfillment. Instead, it is empty. Prophetic secrets comfort people. I think of it like a big plate of spaghetti, which to me is the ultimate comfort food! After you eat it, you no longer feel empty. You feel full and comfortable. That is what prophecy does—it makes you feel full spiritually.

When you prophesy correctly, you are helping to change the condition of society and humanity. You are enabling those who sit in darkness to see the great light of God's love (Matthew 4:16). Prophecy lets the hearers know how much God loves them. It reveals how much He wants to build them up, encourage them, and comfort them. God said that what He created was good (Genesis 1:31). When God sheds prophetic light, it creates something beautiful in your life and in the lives of others who desperately need to know that God is still speaking today.

"THIS IS THAT" SEASON

You may be thinking that you don't have the right manners, social skills, or training to be used powerfully for God. Let me remind you that anyone can learn proper manners and methods to speak for God. Keep in mind that we are in what I like to call a "this is that" season. What does that mean? When the people in Acts began to experience the move of the Holy Spirit, Peter quoted the words of the prophet Joel: "This is that" (Acts 2:16, KJV). What was Peter was talking about? He goes on to say: "Your sons and your daughters shall prophesy, your young men shall see visions, your old men shall dream dreams. And on My menservants and on My maidservants I will pour out My Spirit in those days; and they shall prophesy" (verses 17–18). They will what? Prophesy! We are still living in a "this is that" time! We are living in a time when God's people should prophesy. It should be happening more now than it did then.

We can see in these verses that there really are no age limits or gender requirements for those who can prophesy. It includes women, children, old, and young. I believe God has so much to say that He needs a wide range of vessels to speak for Him. We are in a season when God is using many people from all walks of life as His spokesmen. Don't count yourself out, even if you think you aren't skilled enough to be used this way. If you are young, old, male, or female, Acts 2:16–18 applies to you. It qualifies you to become a well-trained spokesman for the Lord.

Think about it. The Lord spoke to and through children in the Bible. One example was the child Samuel who heard the Lord speak to him three times on one occasion. Young Joseph was just seventeen years old when the secret of the Lord came to him in a dream.

Years ago, a teenager spoke a very powerful word to me when I was looking for a house to rent. He said, "The Lord wants to bless you with something better than what you are looking at." After I heard that, I raised my level of faith and found the best house listed for rent at the time. In Scripture, both old men and old women prophesied. Anna, a prophetess who spoke for God, had been waiting in the temple day and night to see the word concerning the Messiah come to pass.

I believe that Peter was preparing us for a time when there would be an increase in prophecies, causing great acceleration of God's voice speaking to man in the last days. Perhaps because the Lord knew the condition of mankind would grow darker, He needed to increase His voice to mankind. I believe God is letting us know just who He is planning to use—all of us!

I really believe God is saving His best for last. I have always thought that when the Holy Spirit came down on the Day of Pentecost as a rushing, mighty wind, it was because He was in a rush! He was in a hurry to live in us. God was so excited to fill and speak through His born-again people, because it could literally once again be like it was in the Garden of Eden. God had spiritual fellowship with Adam, and that is what we have with the infilling of the Holy Spirit. What used to be in the garden is happening again. God created the best in the garden, and now, in these prophetic last days, His best is being restored. "What has been will be again, what has been done will be done again; there is nothing new under the sun" (Ecclesiastes 1:9, NIV). Not only can we expect God to speak to us the way He did for Adam in the garden, but we can also expect what happened on Pentecost to happen, and it will even be better than they had. God always finishes more powerfully than He starts, and, believe me, He knew how to get off to a powerful start!

In the story of Jesus's first miracle of turning water into wine, the people said that He saved the best wine for last (John 2:10). I can assure you that Jesus is saving the best outpouring of the Holy Spirit for last. The level of prophecies we hear and speak today is going to be more often and more powerful than in the day when Peter stood up to speak.

The Holy Spirit is often likened to a dove. Song of Solomon 2:12 says: "The voice of the turtledove is heard in our land." God's holy dove, His Holy Spirit, has been poured out and is being heard through you and me. In Genesis 8, Noah sent a dove out of the ark three times after the Flood. It was an Old Testament prophetic picture of the Holy Spirit and His work in the earth today.

- *The dove finds no rest.* In verses 8–9, the dove is sent out of the ark and returns after finding no rest. This speaks prophetically of the days of the Old Testament where the Holy Spirit came and spoke through only a few. It also reveals the condition of man without the infilling of the Holy Spirit. The Spirit is looking for a place to rest, a place in which to dwell in human hearts.

- *The dove returned with an olive branch.* In verses 10–11, the dove is once again sent forth, and this time returns with an olive branch. This speaks of the ministry of Jesus, who was filled with the Holy Spirit. Jesus is the olive branch. The dove first rested on Jesus before He rested on us. This is why the testimony of Jesus and prophecy work together. Jesus is first and must be the center of our prophecies.

- *The dove does not return because he finds a place to rest.* In verse 12, the dove was sent out for the final time and didn't return until after the time of the ministry of Jesus. This brings us to the time Peter spoke of on the Day of Pentecost: the "this is that" season! God's Spirit now wants to come and find a place to rest upon your life to speak to you and share His secrets with you. He wants you to be trained and empowered by Him to speak and help others who may be living in darkness, that through the prophetic word of the Lord they may see a great light.

What does this prophetic season mean for us? It means we have to get ready! We have to prepare ourselves to speak for God. God is speaking by His Spirit today. If we will take the time to hear and allow Him to teach us the right methods, we can be confident that we will speak well on His behalf.

Secret Meanings to Reach People

Some people today suggest that we shouldn't have church services that allow the Holy Spirit to move in power and His gifts. They say spiritual gifts or the manifestation of the Holy Spirit may scare the visitors. These same leaders are building their churches without the power of God and His Spirit. This is the opposite of what we found on the Day of Pentecost. There we find the Holy Spirit's power and a lot of visitors! Multitudes heard on that day. Do you know the Bible says that sharing the secrets of God by the unction of the Holy Spirit can be a great way to reach visitors? We do not need to avoid the wonderful person of the Holy Spirit and apologize for Him. Scripture tells us that prophecy needs to be in our churches and is a great way to reach the lost.

> Even so, if unbelievers or people who don't understand these things come into your church meeting and hear everyone speaking in an unknown language, they will think you are crazy. But if all of you are prophesying, and unbelievers or people who don't understand these things come into your meeting, they will be convicted of sin and judged by what you say. As they listen, their secret thoughts will be exposed, and they will fall to their knees and worship God, declaring, "God is truly here among you."
> —1 Corinthians 14:23–25, NLT

My wife and I oversee a very solid, biblical, orderly, Spirit-filled church. The Holy Spirit is our guest in every service, and we want to hear Him speak through the gift of prophecy or any gift of the Spirit He may choose. We believe in allowing the Holy Spirit to move through the congregation and us according to biblical methods and order, because we need His voice in the last days. When people are taught and trained how to function correctly with the things of God, you can allow the Holy Spirit to move, and people will always be blessed. In that setting, you will have great results, and people's lives will be blessed. We need this in the season and time in which we live.

Many churches have gone the other direction, but I want to see churches that flow with an increase of the gifts of the Spirit. Yes, it can be done with the proper training and protocol, but that will not happen if we squelch the voice of the Holy Spirit. Instead of squelching His desire to speak more often, the key is to provide an environment that allows Him to speak with order and proper methods and manners. "Let all things be done decently and in order" (1 Corinthians 14:40).

Contrary to recent popular opinion, the prophetic can be one of the most powerful tools to reach the lost and visitors in our churches. God used the prophetic to reach a visitor in our church one time during a baby dedication when visitors and relatives came and everything was supposed to be nice and visitor friendly. It is the time to be careful not to scare anybody, right? Wrong! I began to pray over the children who were being dedicated, but when I looked up at the audience, through a spiritual vision I saw a word—*suicide*—written over the head of a woman visiting in the service that day. I went to where she sat and told her what I had seen. As soon as I said this, she screamed and cried and fell to the floor. This prophetic word from the Lord given to a visitor may have saved her life. What if I had been trying to be so religiously perpendicular that I failed to let the Holy Spirit share what was on His heart? A life could have been lost!

The multitudes followed Jesus because of the power of God on His life, not because He hid the power of God from them. There is a difference between *flaky ministry* and *powerful anointing*. Because a few have been flaky, we have almost eliminated the legitimate power in a season when God wants to speak the most. Imagine what could happen if we began to use proper manners and methods to allow the Holy Spirit to operate today.

In another incident, the secret of the Lord testified of Jesus and His Spirit. A couple visited a church service at our church, and the young woman had never been around a Spirit-filled church. At first she thought we were strange. It was different to her, and she didn't realize she was being drawn by the anointing of the Holy Spirit. She wanted to leave because it didn't feel like the dead, dry church experience that she had barely attended all her life. But she stayed because she sensed something was drawing her. I heard a name inside my heart peacefully but firmly. So I asked her a question: "Do you know someone by the name of Stacey*?"

She looked shocked and said, "That is my name!" Because I did not want to embarrass anyone, I kept private what the Lord was speaking to me and continued to minister many more things to this couple that they later said no one could have known.

They both said that the things I prophesied had to be God. I showed them scriptures revealing that God speaks, and the prophetic word God spoke through me to this couple was truly a sign to these unbelievers.

I know there are those who misrepresent Jesus and abuse spiritual gifts and the prophetic. However, let's not be afraid and discount or discredit the real simply because of those who abuse the things of God. Prophetic and spiritual gifts are from the Lord and should be used to draw many people to the Lord.

I have had experiences where either the messenger or message was off when someone tried to minister to me. You can find some kind of abuse in just about everything in life if that is all you are focused on. The devil uses spiritual abuses to keep people from the blessings and benefit of the legitimate. This is why I am so grateful I have a great pastor and spiritual father. He helps me rightly divide the words given me. But I have had many wonderful experiences where the real and genuine have been a tremendous blessing in my life.

Like on the Day of Pentecost, often when the Lord begins to demonstrate Himself, people react in the same way they did with Peter in the Upper Room. When Peter stood up to explain what was happening,

---

* Not her real name

the Bible says some began to mock the manifestation of the Holy Spirit while others said, "What is this?" There will always be those who will mock the things of God along with those who will receive. Don't let the mockers stop you from being a spokesman for Him in a day when His words are so needed. As long as your methods are in order, allow the Holy Spirit to speak.

I was once in a church service where a woman who couldn't sing very well (in my opinion) was using the method of singing the word of the Lord to people in the congregation. I must admit that I struggled with this and didn't like it. I had a hard time listening to this woman sing because her voice was not that good. I even think the dogs were howling in the alley behind the church. However, her singing wasn't the real issue, because, truthfully, her methods were in order. In fact, she sang a very accurate word over my life. The funny thing was that after she sang this word to me, I didn't care anymore about her style of singing and ministry. I realized later I had been religiously critical just because I had never seen or experienced such a thing.

In 1 Corinthians 12, which speaks of the nine gifts of the Spirit, the Bible tells us that there will be differences of administration and manifestation of the gifts, but they are all of the same Spirit. Just because we may not like it or have never seen or experienced it doesn't mean it isn't from God—or isn't orderly! Order is represented if the expression of a gift is keeping Jesus as the focus and is being sensitive to the Spirit. The world desperately needs the word of the Lord in this hour. If we work on our manners and methods in the prophetic things of God and are willing to let God speak through us, we can be sure God will touch the life of someone who is lost in darkness.

Be led of His Holy Spirit, and be willing to operate in the legitimate prophetic things of the Spirit. Seek to be an example of the Lord in word and deed, and let God speak through you in these last days when we need His voice the most.

FOUR

LESSONS IN HEARING GOD'S SECRETS

The hearing ear and the seeing eye,
the LORD has made them both.
—Proverbs 20:12

P-*A-G-A-D-O!* I HEARD MYSELF SPELL OUT EACH LETTER OF this word as they appeared in a spiritual vision. One by one I saw the letters appear across the wall of the Spanish-speaking church where I was ministering. I said each letter and waited for the translator to speak what I was seeing.

I don't speak Spanish fluently, and at that time I knew far less than I do now. I definitely didn't know what *pagado* meant. So I was feeling very unsure about what I was seeing and spelling since I hadn't heard this word before. As soon as the translator finished repeating what I was saying, everyone in the crowd was jumping, crying, and praising God. I stood there trying to understand what I saw in the vision and why everyone was shouting. I asked the translator, "What is happening, and why are they so excited?"

The translator began to explain what was happening. "They are excited because you just spelled in Spanish the word *pagado*, which means *paid* in English! We are believing for our church to be built debt free, and it will cost millions to do it!"

I rejoiced with them and thanked the Lord that He had just given them a sign. The pastor later told me he believed God for a specific word of confirmation about the building project. He had asked the Lord to confirm if they were to build the church debt free. He took this revealed secret as a word of confirmation from heaven and paid for a multimillion-dollar building in cash—debt free.

The word I saw is just one way that God communicates. God has designed us to hear through the "hearing ear" and the "seeing eye" according to Proverbs 20:12. In other words, He has many ways of communicating. This verse isn't just talking about the natural ear and eye but also the spiritual ear and eye. This is why Jesus often said: "He who has an ear, let him hear what the Spirit says" (Revelation 2:29). Everyone He was talking to had ears, but He was speaking to their spiritual ears, telling them that they needed to hear the secret things of the Spirit.

THREE WAYS A SECRET COMES

Throughout this book, we have seen that God desires to speak and is still speaking. I believe that by now you are getting hungry to hear from God.

When God reveals a secret, it can come in very practical ways through natural events or circumstances. He also speaks in spiritual ways through things like spiritual visions, dreams, impressions, and an inward witness of the Holy Spirit. At times, God may also communicate to us through our five senses of hearing, seeing, tasting, smelling, and feeling, even though our natural senses are not God's primary way of communication. We must remember that God is not a human being; He is a Spirit being as Jesus told us in John 4:24. However, He knows how to get His message across to us and get past our human limitations.

In this chapter we will examine the different ways that God speaks to us. When He communicates, God's communication usually falls under one of three basic categories:

1. Hearing

2. Seeing

3. Feeling

When I was first learning how God communicates, I felt like I couldn't hear, see, or feel anything. In my frustration for God to communicate to me, I once spent most of an evening praying. I spent a lot of that time complaining that I couldn't hear from Him and telling Him that His ways of communicating were too hard! I had lain down on the floor and started to fall asleep when I heard some words ring in my heart. It wasn't in my head but in my heart; it seemed right in the middle of my abdomen. I heard these words: "Hank, My ability to communicate to you is greater than your inability to hear. I have many different ways to communicate My heart and voice to you!"

That day changed my life because I realized God has many different ways to speak to me.

The best example of how God speaks to us through three basic categories is Jesus. He revealed the will of His Father through what He heard, saw, and felt.

- *Hearing*—"All things that I heard from My Father I have made known to you" (John 15:15).

- *Seeing*—"The Son can do nothing of Himself, but what He sees the Father do" (John 5:19).

- *Feeling or sensing*—"When Jesus perceived that they were about to come and take Him by force to make Him king, He departed again to the mountain by Himself alone" (John 6:15).

God communicated to and through the apostle Paul in these same three ways of hearing, seeing, and sensing (also called perceiving).

- *Hearing*—The apostle Paul heard the Lord's voice: "Saul, Saul, why are you persecuting Me?" (Acts 9:4).

- *Seeing*—Paul saw visions in the night (Acts 16:9; 18:9).

- *Feeling or sensing*—Paul was vexed in his spirit and felt uneasy in his heart about what a young lady was saying to him (Acts 16:17–18).

There are other scriptural examples of these three ways that God communicates His secrets. He may communicate to you by all three or by just one or two of the three. The key is not to give up or be discouraged. Keep listening, and keep asking Him to communicate to you. In time, you will learn to hear, see, and sense. Here are some more scriptural examples of the three ways God communicates:

Isaiah 21:2–3

- *Hearing*—"I was distressed when I heard it" (verse 3).

- *Seeing*—"A distressing vision is declared to me" (verse 2).

- *Feeling or sensing*—"Therefore my loins are filled with pain" (verse 3).

Revelation 10:1, 4, 10

- *Hearing*—"I heard a voice from heaven saying to me…" (verse 4).

- *Seeing*—"I saw still another mighty angel" (verse 1).

- *Feeling or sensing*—"I took the little book out of the angel's hand and ate it, and it was as sweet as honey in my mouth" (verse 10).

This pattern is also evident at the birth of the early church into a powerful, supernatural one on the Day of Pentecost. Notice the pattern found in Acts 2:

- *Hearing*—"A sound from heaven, as of a rushing mighty wind" (verse 2).

- *Seeing*—"There appeared to them divided tongues, as of fire, and one sat upon each of them" (verse 3).

- *Sensing*—"It [the wind] filled the whole house where they were sitting" (verse 2).

As we have seen in these examples, when the Lord communicates with us, it is by hearing, seeing, and sensing. Normally God communicates in this way through our *spiritual* senses. These senses cause us to hear God through things like spiritual and open visions, dreams, a still small voice, the inward witness, and the voice of the Holy Spirit. The following examples from Scripture help us to better understand the five spiritual senses:

- *Spiritual hearing*—God spoke a word into Samuel's spirit (1 Samuel 9:15–16).

- *Spiritual seeing*—The servant saw in the spirit realm (2 Kings 6:17).

- *Spiritual touch*—Jeremiah's mouth was touched with the words of the Lord (Jeremiah 1:9).

- *Spiritual taste*—Through spiritual discernment, the sons of the prophets spiritually tasted that there was poison in the pot (2 Kings 4:40).

- *Spiritual smell*—Jesus delivered a man with a foul spirit (Mark 9:25). When something smells bad, we will refer to it as foul. Jesus could discern what spirit was in this man perhaps by what He spiritually smelled or discerned in the spirit.

Of course, the last three spiritual senses listed above fall under the category of feeling or sensing, while the others are simply hearing and seeing. All of these spiritual senses can be developed as we continue to press into the things of God, and exercise and develop them: "Those who by reason of use have their senses exercised to discern both good and evil" (Hebrews 5:14). This verse is speaking about the development of our spiritual senses.

There are also the five natural senses of hearing, seeing, smelling, tasting, and touching, which are used for natural things. God also speaks in the natural realm on the earth through the circumstances of normal, everyday life, which we experience with our five physical senses. He can speak through specific events and through nature. Of course, we shouldn't depend on natural hearing over listening to God in the Spirit, but God can and does speak in the natural realm at times. However, our natural senses can work in conjunction with our spiritual senses.

Once we understand that God does speak in both the spiritual realm and the natural realm, using both our spiritual and natural senses, it will help us learn to hear Him more effectively. John 12:28–29 gives us an example of God speaking in these two realms: "'Father, glorify Your name.' Then a voice came from heaven, saying, 'I have both glorified it and will glorify it again.' Therefore the people who stood by and heard it said that it had thundered. Others said, 'An angel has spoken to Him.'"

First, God spoke a specific word that Jesus heard clearly because He heard God in the Spirit. Then there were those who heard or associated God's voice with natural thunder. Others thought it was an angel or perceived that it was something of the spiritual realm like an angel. I believe God wanted everyone to hear Him, but the truth is the people didn't correctly hear or perceive His voice. Nevertheless, God's voice still touched both the spiritual and natural realms when He communicated.

SUPERSPIRITUAL HEARING

If we really want to hear from God, His voice will come, but it is important that we don't always look for the loud, thunderous things to validate God's voice to us. We don't want to misinterpret His voice or interpret everything as God speaking when in fact it might really just be thunder or lightning.

When I was first saved and just out of high school, two friends and I went to a conference. As young bachelors, we had little money, and we shared a hotel room to save expenses. In the middle of the night, one of the guys woke us up. He was whispering loudly and pointing in the direction of the closet and staring at a white glowing object in the closet. I insisted it was nothing, but our friend was sure it was an angel or some type of spirit being. He began to speak to it, telling it to identify itself. I admit we were young and overzealous in many ways. Yet, there seemed to be something to this white object, for it was moving side to side.

Finally I got up to turn the light on to see what this *angel* thing was. It was just as I thought. It was a white shirt being blown back and forth by the air conditioner, and the slight glow came from the streetlight outside. Again, sometimes it might be supernatural and other times just thunder—or a white shirt!

When hearing the secrets of the Lord, let your main focus be to glorify the Lord, not just to look for the spooky and spectacular. As we saw in John 12:28, it was when Jesus demonstrated His desire to glorify God and bring honor to Him that the voice of His Father came. If our motive is to truly glorify the Lord through the prophetic, and not just use it for an opportunity to push for our own glory, we will hear the voice of God more clearly just as Jesus did.

Now that we have established the fact that God uses both our spiritual and natural senses to speak, I want to give you the avenues through which you will begin to hear, see, and sense His voice.

Hearing comes through:

- *Prophecy*—We hear the word of the Lord spoken to us and to others.

- *The inner voice of the Holy Spirit*—We hear His still, small voice inside our hearts.

- *Hearing the Bible spoken*—God will often quicken a verse to us.

- *Tongues and interpretation of tongues*—We hear His word to us.

Seeing comes through:

- Visions and dreams (Acts 2:17)

- Visitations of angels (Acts 27:23)

Sensing/feeling or perceiving comes through:

- *Inner peace*—We are to pursue peace (Psalm 34:14).

- *Perceiving* (Acts 8:23; 17:22; 27:10)

- *Being grieved in your spirit*—uneasy or sensing something is not right (Acts 16:18)

- *Spiritual senses exercised*—through spiritual discernment (Hebrews 5:14)

PROPHECY: THE VEHICLE OF GOD'S SECRETS

God is not only looking for people who can hear, see, and sense His voice, but He also needs those who can share His prophetic secrets. One of the most prominent ways we will communicate for God is through the avenue of prophecy. This is what Paul said when speaking to the Corinthian church. He said we could all exhort, edify, and bring a comforting word through prophecy (1 Corinthians 14:39). This means we can build up, cheer up, and help up people through the means of prophecy.

You might be asking, "Just what is prophecy?" Prophecy, in its simple sense, is the heart and mind of God being communicated to man or the world, usually by something seen, heard, or felt. In the Hebrew, *prophecy* is *chazah* (*khaw-zaw*), which means "to mentally perceive and to have a vision of." We must remember that prophecy, or God communicating to man, starts with an inspiration from God. When we prophesy, we speak or write a word inspired by the Lord, and that word will generally come to us through hearing, seeing, or sensing.

Because prophecy is God speaking to us through an inspired vessel, we should desire for prophecy to operate. Prophecy is a good thing, not a bad thing. Just because some have mistreated prophecy does not mean we should eliminate it. We should desire it to manifest, but not just that; we should desire it to manifest through us!

You see, desire is one of the best ways to bring the secrets of God to your life. First Corinthians 14:1 says, "Desire spiritual gifts, but especially that you may prophesy." We are told not to despise prophecy in 1 Thessalonians 5:20. This means we shouldn't despise hearing from God and ministering prophetically to others.

I find prophecy to be helpful and necessary, especially when I was going through difficult times in trying to find the road God wanted for me in the ministry. The Lord used many prophetic people and prophecies to help encourage, confirm, and reveal what God had for my wife and me. They were incredible revelations spoken straight from God through different individuals for our lives.

When God shares a secret He wants you to prophesy, it can come spontaneously, or, at other times, it may come to you as building revelation over time until you share it. These secrets can come to us to reveal the past, present, and future. Prophecy isn't just limited to confirmation.

Several years before I actually started to pastor, I received a prophecy from a valid minister who prophesied that I was going to pastor. I thought this person absolutely missed it, because I had no leading from God whatsoever to pastor a church. This word wasn't a confirmation, but it proved later to be a future word revealed to me that I am walking in joyously today!

Let's look at Scripture to better understand that prophetic words can be present, future, or past.

- *Present example of a prophetic word*—In John 4, Jesus told the woman at the well that she was *presently* living with a man who wasn't her husband.

- *Future example of a prophetic word*—In Acts 11:28, the prophet Agabus prophesied about a great famine that would come upon the earth in a *future* time.

- *Past example of a prophetic word*—In John 4:18, Jesus tells the woman that she had had five husbands in the *past*.

Another example of prophecy not having to necessarily confirm something to you but rather reveal something new is when Jesus prophesied to Peter how he would die. This was not a confirming word to Peter about his own death but rather a future word being prophetically spoken. (See John 21:18.) Prophecy—whether present, future, or past—is to bring the heart of God and His secrets as a blessing to this generation. It is the primary way we communicate to others what we are hearing, sensing, and seeing.

Because of the Holy Spirit's grace, which we enjoy as the children of God, we are no longer limited to just a few who heard God and prophesied, as we see in the Old Testament. We can all prophesy. It is helpful to understand that you don't always have to understand the prophecy when you prophesy for God. This is a common misconception when it comes to the prophetic. People think that because you prophesied it, you automatically know what it means. No, you are just reporting what you have heard, seen, or perceived.

Think of a prophecy like a news report; it is relaying information, not giving your personal insight into the situation. Prophetic secrets are often mysteries or riddles when they are received and even shared. Often you may not understand in human terms what it is that the Lord is trying to communicate. For example, the apostle Peter didn't understand the vision that he received of the Lord in Acts 10. He didn't jump up from that place and say, "Wow, now I have it!" The truth of the thing developed in him over time.

The Lord communicates at times in riddles or mysteries so we will seek Him further for the meaning of the message. This is why Enoch heard God. He wasn't any different from most, except that he walked in a very dedicated way with God. The more we do this, like Enoch we will be taken into realms of God's nature we have never been to before!

WHIRLWINDS, FIERY TRIALS, AND EARTH-SHAKING MOMENTS

Prophecy can be the very thing that will pull you through some of your worst trials. Have you ever felt like you were walking through a whirlwind, fiery trial, or some earth-shaking moment in life? I believe this is why the Bible states that the purpose of prophecy is for edification, exhortation, and comfort. It is because a word prophetically spoken can pull us through difficult times.

When my wife, Brenda, and I were newly married, we needed a major financial miracle of several thousands of dollars, which we did not have. A prophetic word spoken to us by a minister we didn't know pulled us through that trial. It came when we were attending an out-of-town meeting, and nobody knew our situation. That night, the guest speaker prophesied that a financial miracle would come in an unexpected way from an unexpected source very soon. That's all the word said.

That word was spoken in April of that year, and later in the same year, on Halloween night, we stopped by our post office box after work. Inside was an envelope from someone in a different state with whom we were only briefly acquainted. That person sent a check that paid off all our debt. Thank God for His prophetic word in our fiery trial, whirlwind, and shaking moment; it pulled us through.

However, it is not just prophecies given to us from others that we can depend on to give us strength. What happens if there is no one around to give you a prophecy? Then you can use your own ability to hear God's secrets to pull yourself through. Do you know that is one of the best things you can learn to do as a Christian? If there is no one available to prophesy to you, then you must know how to find God's voice for yourself.

This is exactly what happened to the prophet Elijah in 1 Kings 19. He was looking for the Lord to speak to him during a difficult, lonely time. It seemed so bad to him that we find him requesting that he might die (verse 4). Elijah experienced all three phenomena—he had the earthquake, the whirlwind, and even some fire. As a result, he looked for God's voice in these things, but it could not be found.

Sometimes it's hard to hear God in the midst of a storm. Then we tend to expect God to speak in a stormy way just because of what we are experiencing. That is why I believe God didn't speak to Elijah through those elements. Sometimes you have to get away from the storm to hear God in the way He wants to talk to you, not just the way you want to hear Him! You need to find a quiet place where you can hear the whisper of God's voice. God spoke to Elijah in the still, small voice, but would Elijah have heard it with his mind caught up in the whirlwind? Probably not!

Even if no one is available to give you that life-changing prophecy, you can still hear God. Get alone, get quiet, and stop screaming for God to speak to you in the midst of your storm. When you calm down and listen, taking your mind off the fiery trial and your earth-shaking moment, you will start to hear, see, and sense the Lord. It may not be in the earth-shattering method you hoped, but you will hear Him if you settle down and listen. This example of Elijah gives hope that no matter what we face, God is waiting to communicate to us through something heard, seen, or perceived. We have to wait in the quiet, and we will find that His still, small voice is available in our most challenging times.

STRETCH YOUR EYES

If we want to see in the spirit more accurately, we need to simply ask the Lord to help our ability to see Him. Elisha and his servant faced a very challenging situation (2 Kings 6). They were outnumbered by the Syrian army, and it looked hopeless. One powerful prophetic prayer—"LORD, I pray, open his eyes that he may see"—changed everything (verse 17). In the natural realm, his servant could only see the armies of Syria. When Elisha prayed for the Lord to open his servant's eyes, it was in reference to seeing in the spiritual realm. How were his spiritual eyes opened? By asking the Lord for it. God did in fact open his eyes as we are told in Scripture. Once his eyes were opened, he saw the horses and chariots from the heavenly army of God.

God wants your eyes to be opened in the spirit. Seeing in the spirit realm prophetically gives you heaven's perspective regarding the situations you might face. We can also have our eyes opened in the spirit through dreams and visions. Peter stood up on the Day of Pentecost, declaring that in the last days God would give visions and dreams. Dreams are a great way for the Lord to communicate His heart and will because they often occur when we are not awake and trying to apply our natural perspective to things. While we are awake, we often are restless and worried and have a harder time being still in God.

Sometimes before I minister I pray in the Spirit and allow myself to fall asleep while praying. Now, I am not saying we are to be lazy and fall asleep in prayer! However, after a quality time of prayer, I will fall asleep, and often the Lord will speak by opening my spiritual eyes.

For example, while I pray, the Lord may show me something about a person to whom I haven't spoken in a while, and, when I contact that person, it proves to be right. At other times the Lord has shown me things about people that I wasn't to act upon but only pray for them. This is where good spiritual discipline and a good pastor will help you walk through your learning process.

I like to refer to the process of having our spiritual eyes opened as *listening with our eyes*. Yes, we can learn to receive the secrets of God by learning to listen with our eyes. God will show you things with your spiritual eyes. I like to keep my spiritual eyes open to things the Lord may be saying to me. I try to keep myself in a place of watching as I go about my day.

I am not talking about walking around with some strange spiritual stare. I once knew a person who used to gaze off into heaven as if to receive some heavenly vision. The problem was that even if he did receive something, he looked foolish and weird. It was hard for people to take him and his message seriously. Little things like this that draw attention to yourself will hinder you. Just be normal and real.

I can *hear with my eyes* by keeping my spiritual *focus* on the people or situations to which God may be calling me to minister. It may be my church members, so I place my vision toward them and see what I will hear. I have found that when my eyes are focused, God may even reveal things unrelated to my area of focus.

When I was writing my book *Don't Leave God Alone*, I was typing away but watching to see if the Lord would show me anything.[1] I was working but listening with my eyes. One day as I was looking at the computer monitor, suddenly a person's face flashed very quickly before me. I saw a lady in my church who was due to have a baby any day. I immediately asked the Lord if He wanted to say anything to me about her. After all, why did I see her face? I had not been thinking of her right then. The Lord spoke to my heart and said, "She will have the baby Tuesday night into Wednesday morning."

"Wow!" I thought. "Today is Monday, so that means tomorrow into

Wednesday she will have this baby." I gave this message to them on Monday, but Tuesday and Wednesday came and went with no baby. I didn't know why God showed me this or said what He said. To all of our surprise, the following week, Tuesday night into Wednesday, she had her baby. It was just a week later. We have to be careful not to quit trusting the word or misinterpret things when it doesn't look like it is happening the way we expected. However, because I was watching, God was willing to speak through my eyes.

Another way I increase my spiritual seeing is to *stretch my eyes*. Now I don't mean take your natural eyes and stretch them. I am talking about stretching your spiritual eyes. While praying, I will often quiet down and ask the Lord to show me something He wants to reveal. By stretching my eyes, I am stretching my faith and believing I will receive something specific. It is a stretch of faith.

In one conference where I was ministering, I knew there would be several thousand in attendance, but I wanted to stretch my eyes of faith for anything God may want to do for individuals. I was expecting it! As I spoke, the Holy Spirit began to show me that to my left in the very back row of the meeting there was a man sitting there to whom I was to minister. God will often have a specific anointing or purpose for an individual in a prophetic setting. Remember that as Jesus ministered, the power of the Lord was present to heal everyone in the room (Luke 5:17).

In the case of this conference, the Lord had already shown me this man in my spirit ahead of the meeting. I acted on what I had stretched my eyes of faith for earlier. In the meeting, the Lord began to describe the man I had seen in my hotel room and even spoke his name to me supernaturally. I began to describe where this man was sitting. A man with the exact name came running forward from that exact location I had seen earlier in prayer. The Lord ministered to this person in a great way because I *stretched my eyes* to see whom God wanted to specifically touch that day. Stretch your seeing by using your faith.

The key to seeing or listening with our spiritual eyes is really just to become sensitive by staying in fellowship with the Lord throughout the day. Literally, it is *keeping your eyes lifted up*! This is what Jesus did when He raised Lazarus from the dead in John 11. The Bible says Jesus lifted His eyes to His heavenly Father. In other words, He was dependent on His Father and kept in constant intimate fellowship. All He had to do was raise His eyes and the Father would respond. This is exactly how to have the Lord respond to you. Keep your eyes lifted up.

CIRCUMCISE YOUR EARS

Not only do we need to practice stretching our eyes, but we also need to increase our hearing. If we want to sharpen our hearing ear to the secrets of God, then we must have our ears circumcised. Of course, I am not saying that you literally cut skin away from your ear. It is not natural circumcision but a spiritual one.

> To whom shall I speak and give warning,
> That they may hear?
> Indeed their ear is uncircumcised,
> And they cannot give heed.
> Behold, the word of the LORD is a reproach to them;
> They have no delight in it.
> —JEREMIAH 6:10

This kind of circumcision deals with cutting away the nature of sin that can affect our heart or ability to hear the Lord. The circumcision of our ear means we need to cut away the things of the world that dominate our hearing. This is why it is so vital to make sure the things we listen to are pure and not defiled by the things of this world. The more you allow your ears to hear the world's perspective, the more it will hinder your spiritual hearing. Constantly listening to the world's programming, music, and input will cause your spiritual hearing to become dull to the Holy Spirit. In this verse in Jeremiah, God wanted to talk to someone, but He was looking for those who had an ear circumcised from the fleshly ways of this world. These people couldn't listen correctly because they had too much flesh obstructing their ability to hear from God. As a result they didn't even delight in the word of the Lord—they were more interested and comfortable hearing fleshly things.

We must continually give our ears to the Bible and to spiritual things. This will help us hear and share the secrets of the Lord with more purity and maturity. We can have a true circumcised spiritual ear that hears the words of God if we will first start with our heart motive.

If you want sharp hearing in the spirit, you must ask yourself what you are truly ready to cut away from your life. What you minister to others is greatly affected by a life of purity or impurity. We read in Acts 21:9 that Philip had four virgin daughters who prophesied. Prophetically speaking, their virginity speaks of purity. In other words the prophetic and purity must go together.

Look also at Jeremiah 4:4: "Circumcise yourselves to the LORD, and take away the foreskins of your hearts." This verse is reminding us that we need to remove the excess things in our hearts that prevent us from wanting to keep a pure spiritual ear. In Romans 2:29, the Bible tells us, "Circumcision is that of the heart, in the Spirit, not in the letter; whose praise is not from men but from God." For the Christian, circumcision is something we do in a spiritual sense. We should want to cut away things that are sinful and fleshly because we love God and want to do what is honorable to Him.

What we allow our ears to hear or our hearts to receive will form certain mind-sets in our walk with God. Keeping our hearts spiritually circumcised protects our ears, eyes, and hearts from becoming defiled. Our ears, eyes, and hearts are gates that will open either to the influence of the Lord or to the evils of this world. When you protect these gates by walking pure before the Lord, it improves your ability to receive His secrets. Samson lost his eyes, for example, because he didn't protect his gates. He let his eyes look toward compromise, and eventually his eyes literally were poked out. It represents to us that if we allow our eye and ear gates to compromise, we run the risk of losing our spiritual seeing and hearing. It will ultimately destroy our anointing.

Others have had their ears cut off by either their own actions or by the influence of others. Do you remember Malchus, the man who lost his ear when Peter cut it off in the Garden of Gethsemane? (See John 18:10.) In an instant, he lost his ear. While this was a natural event, we can still gain a spiritual principle from it. After Peter cut off this man's ear, Jesus reached up and restored his ear, enabling him to be able to hear again. Without question, I believe the Lord is restoring our hearing, which is our ability to understand His voice even when it seems it has been cut off.

Eli, a priest of the Lord, became spiritually dull to the things of God because of compromise, and eventually became dull in hearing the Lord. You can study his life in the first few chapters of 1 Samuel. The Bible tells us that in his time, there was no open vision (1 Samuel 3:1). Could it be that God's voice was cut off because of Eli's compromise? Certainly! So the Lord had to restore His voice through a pure young child named Samuel who became a powerful prophet. Even when the Lord began to speak to Samuel during his childhood, Eli couldn't immediately tell it was the Lord calling out to the boy.

Eli remained cut off from the Lord and couldn't spiritually discern or sense the voice of the Lord when it was spoken. The Bible says that Eli's eyes "had begun to grow so dim that he could not see" (1 Samuel 3:2). Of course, naturally speaking, he was old, but I also believe the Bible drew attention to his condition as a priest, which had become compromised. The Bible gives us some definite indicators that Eli had allowed compromise to adversely affect his priesthood.

His discernment was dulled:

1. *1 Samuel 1:13–15*—He thought that Hannah was drunk when she was in intense prayer.

2. *1 Samuel 3*—As the priest, Eli was not quick to realize that it was the Lord calling Samuel.

He allowed temple compromise:

1. *1 Samuel 2:22*—He allowed his sons to sexually seduce the women who attended the door of the temple. Thus, Eli failed to protect the temple from sin.

2. *1 Samuel 2:27–36*—He allowed his sons to use temple money for their own pleasures, thereby dishonoring the sacrificial offerings of the people.

Eli and his sons made themselves "fat with the best of all the offerings of Israel My people" (1 Samuel 2:29). As a result, his house would be cut off and his family would all live in poverty, begging in the temple (1 Samuel 2:32–36).

Sharpening our hearing means that we will have to purify what we choose to listen to and make certain we are attending to God's voice in prayer, in His Word, and inside of our spirit. Don't allow compromise to make you dull of hearing God's voice. Tune your ear and you will hear Him clearly.

THE THREE SECRET-KILLERS

In 1 John 2:16, three fleshly sins are identified—the lust of the eyes, the lust of the flesh, and the pride of life. These behaviors will cut off our ability to see, hear, and perceive in the Spirit.

The lust of the eyes will interfere with our ability to see God. Instead, we will be busy looking at things that God doesn't want us to see or be focused on. When we make the things we see our primary focus, thus appealing to our natural flesh, we will develop spiritual scales over our eyes that will hinder us from seeing in the spiritual realm.

Second, the lust of the flesh is dangerous because it can cause us to hunger for things contrary to the things of the Spirit. When we hunger for the wrong things, we won't discern or perceive situations correctly. We can't tell right from wrong or the true from the false because our flesh desires the wrong things. When our flesh is lusting for the wrong things, we cannot properly sense God in the spirit. Fleshly lust is not necessarily sexual lust; it can be any distraction, busy schedule, or excessive interests outside of the Lord.

The pride of life is evident when we allow the voice of self-exaltation to speak to us. When we are so busy praising and making a place for ourselves, we can't hear God speak. It clogs our spiritual hearing because we are too busy singing the praises of self. Many prophetic people are caught up in this syndrome. They want to receive the applause for the things they prophesy and do, and they often push their way to make a place for their platform. Many prophesy from this motive. They are more concerned about being heard than about the Lord being heard.

The lust of the eyes, the lust of the flesh, and the boastful pride of life are killers of the prophetic secrets of God. These are the things the devil used against Jesus in the wilderness as He was fasting and praying in Matthew 4.

The devil began his temptations by using the lust of the flesh against Jesus. He tempted Him by telling Him to command the stones to be turned to bread. He knew Jesus was fasting and hungry. Jesus could have easily satisfied His flesh. Instead, Jesus kept His hunger upon God and His word.

The next thing Satan used was the boastful pride of life. He wanted Jesus to do something foolish, like throw Himself off the pinnacle of the temple, expecting God to save Him. This is what I call *the boastful pride of life*. Today some people do ridiculous things in order to prove they have some kind of prophetic power. I have seen people interrupt services and rudely start ministering to people so they can be recognized. These people are absorbed with themselves.

The devil also used the lust of the eyes to try to get Jesus off track.

He showed Him all the kingdoms of the world and told Jesus to bow down and worship him. The devil wanted Jesus to look at all the world could offer, but Jesus didn't give in to that! The devil still tries this today. He was enticing Jesus with the lust of the eyes. He does the same with many people who have good intentions. He will try to get your eyes on something other than the Lord.

When you keep your heart in the right place and position yourself to focus on the Lord, you can expect to hear the secrets of the Lord. A life of purity will be a life filled with God's secrets. Use your faith to hear the secrets of God. If you have not found the opportunity to prophesy recently, ask the Lord to open doors for you. You can learn to hear and prophesy in the privacy of your own room, and this is the best place to start. Then test your hearing and ability to prophesy with members of your family. My wife and I prophesy to one another. We love doing that. From there, allow God to open doors for you to minister His secrets in other places and to other individuals. If you keep your heart right and do not seek personal position or promotion, then God will make a place for you to minister His secrets. Don't push for your place, keep your heart pure, and expect the Lord to make room for you to share the secrets of the Lord.

F I V E

PROPHETIC BOUNDARIES

The secret of the LORD is with those who fear
Him, and He will show them His covenant.

—Psalm 25:14

S OME TIME AGO, WHILE MY WIFE AND I WERE MINISTERING
at a church, we had gone to dinner with the host pastors and
associates. While we were eating, a couple who had been seated
at an adjacent table got up to leave and stopped by our table. The woman
said she had overheard us talking about the Lord and ministry. She
started to speak to us in an odd prophetic sort of way, attempting to tell
us things about our lives. She only addressed the men at the table and
seemed to feel the need to put her hand on our shoulders, which she
kept doing repeatedly. That was an immediate warning signal to me that
something wasn't right. She was overbearing and kept hanging around
our table, acting as if she was called to be a voice into our ministries.

She was loud and brash and continued to explain how God used her
in the prophetic in her own church in another state. Here was the worst
part of it: she and her husband had just had several drinks, as we could
see by the many leftover beer bottles on their table. So, by the time she

made her way to our table and interrupted our conversation, she was not entirely sober. She had no clue that all she was doing was embarrassing herself. I believe the pastor of the church she claimed to be part of would be horrified had he seen her behavior. The truth is, she either caused her pastor plenty of headaches, or she didn't attend there enough to be considered a member.

Usually people like this are undisciplined, unchurched, or attend church only on their own terms. They think they have a prophetic gift and the right to use it whenever they wish, even half drunk!

We remained polite but kept our conversation to a minimum, hoping she would leave. However, she didn't get the idea that we weren't interested in her "prophetic" input. It was sad to watch her trying to be prophetic while she was slurring her speech.

You are probably as horrified as we were as you read this. But some people handle the prophetic things of God in this same way while they are sober. They walk up to strangers, interrupt them at restaurants, and can't take the hint that their listeners are not interested. They interrupt church services where they are just visiting. They expect the pastor to give them a platform, even though the pastor has never met them and has had no time to see what kind of life they live. They like to give people secretive prophecies, and they want little accountability in their "gifting." They make a special point of letting everyone know they are called and gifted to pray and prophesy.

If they attend a church, they feel they should be recognized as a spiritual voice of some kind, but they usually don't want to follow any type of prophetic guidelines the church has established. In fact, many of them feel that because they have a "message from God" they aren't subject to anyone. Instead, they think the pastor and the people should be subject to their message.

I call this type of behavior *a lack of prophetic boundaries*. These "prophets" or "intercessors" are just plain immature believers who are a detriment to the kingdom of God and the church. Contrary to what some believe, people in the Bible who ministered in the prophetic secrets of God used proper accountability, manners, and protocol. I want to give some specifics on accountability and proper boundaries in the prophetic in this chapter.

ESTABLISHING BOUNDARIES

Because everyone is at a different level in receiving the secrets of the Lord, the boundary lines may seem to vary from person to person and situation to situation. Boundaries of ministry will also vary from church to church. For this reason, I don't think people who are visiting a church should stand up to prophesy in that church. They need to first understand how that pastor runs the service and how he accommodates people who prophesy.

People who are not representing a holy lifestyle by their actions should not prophesy, as was the case of the woman who stopped by to prophesy to us at our table. She was inconsiderate in the way she interrupted us, she did not use good social manners, and she was only drawn to the men at the table. In the example I gave earlier of the time my wife and I went up to the couple at the table, we were considerate of their time, we were walking right with God, and we used proper manners by making sure they wanted us to keep talking to them. Their receptivity and desire to be filled with the Holy Spirit were fruit, demonstrating that we were handling the situation correctly.

This is why the apostle Paul instructed us to minister the gifts in decency and order, as well as in love (1 Corinthians 14:40). He was addressing the church at Corinth, which historically was a very undisciplined, carnal, disruptive, out-of-order, and immature church. In 1 Corinthians, Paul addressed many problems needing to be put back in proper order in that church, which we see today not only in our churches but also outside the local church. Yet in 1 Corinthians we learn more about spiritual gifts than in any other book in the Bible. It usually is not the majority of people who handle the prophetic things of God improperly; rather, it is the few who make it bad for everyone else.

Paul told this prophetic, Spirit-filled, and spiritually gifted church of believers to let everything be done in decency and order. Why did he have to say this? We can see the reason in the opening words of this letter to the church at Corinth. In 1 Corinthians 1:6–7, Paul confirms that these believers had the testimony of Christ and even spiritual gifts: "...even as the testimony of Christ was confirmed in you, so that you come short in no gift." Yet in the following verses, Paul had to address some things that were out of order in their testimonies of Christ and the gifts:

> Now I plead with you, brethren, by the name of our Lord Jesus Christ, that you all speak the same thing, and that there be no divisions among you, but that you be perfectly joined together in the same mind and in the same judgment. For it has been declared to me concerning you, my brethren, by those of Chloe's household, that there are contentions among you.
> —1 CORINTHIANS 1:10–11

History indicates that Paul spent about three years with this church, trying to bring them to a place of spiritual maturity. (See Acts 18:11, 18.) The Corinthians had the spiritual gifts but had many issues that needed correction when it came to their behavior. Below are some of the examples of issues Paul spoke to the church at Corinth about:

- *Carnal fleshly behavior*—1 Corinthians 2

- *Immorality and carnality*—1 Corinthians 3

- *Unfaithfulness and lack of dependability*—1 Corinthians 4

- *Immoral issues*—1 Corinthians 5

- *Legal issues and carnal issues*—1 Corinthians 6

- *Marriage issues*—1 Corinthians 7

- *Murmuring and complaining*—1 Corinthians 10

- *Strife issues*—1 Corinthians 11

- *Disorder, competition, and interrupting each other*—1 Corinthians 12

You can see from these examples that this church had many behavioral problems and needed to understand moral and righteous boundaries. In that mix, they also had to learn ministry boundaries in the church setting. It was because of all these issues that Paul had to set proper order to those who desired to operate in spiritual gifts and prophecy. This order was not to eliminate the spiritual gifts or keep the people from ministering in them. It was to establish the necessary standards so that the church could truly be blessed by such gifts. Often people who want to operate in the secrets of God forget or ignore this side of things. We can understand from these examples of Paul to the church of Corinth that gifting without character, morals, guidelines, and proper order leads to a mess!

Notice that Paul, as the overseer of this church, was establishing order. He was making sure things were being done and accounted for correctly. He wasn't trying to control or squelch the ministry of spiritual gifts. Instead, he was establishing boundaries. This is why I encourage pastors and leaders to teach, train, and instruct the people they lead. Pastors should teach their people the proper order for sharing a prophecy from the Lord. The people in attendance should know that they cannot undermine the guidelines the pastor has set up if they are only a visitor and have not had time to learn them. New members should take the time to understand and accept the boundaries for ministering in the spiritual gifts that their pastor has established. These boundaries will vary from church to church.

If the pastor of the church you attend simply does not allow people in the congregation to prophesy, then you will have to accept that boundary if that is going to be your church home. If he doesn't allow visitors to prophesy, which I generally don't allow either, then you will have to abide by that. If he only allows those who have gone through some type of prophetic training to do it, then you need to follow through and honor his boundaries in love and with a supportive attitude.

LEADERS LEAD

Leaders need to do as Ephesians 4 says: equip the people to do the work of the ministry and bring them into maturity. Where leadership and order are undefined, people will do what is right by their own standards. "In those days there was no king in Israel; everyone did what was right in his own eyes" (Judges 21:25). It is vital for leaders to teach people how to minister correctly inside and outside the church walls. As people, we need to learn how to correctly behave. We should be willing to submit our gifts to spiritual leaders who can give an account for our gifting and character. Paul wrote in his letter to Timothy that he should "know how [he] ought to conduct [himself] in the house of God" (1 Timothy 3:15). That is advice that every believer needs to follow.

Boundaries are not established so the gifts can be controlled and squelched but rather so that they have an orderly channel through which to function. Proper boundaries can actually make room for the gifts to operate. When people understand protocol, they have the tools with which to work.

When Jesus performed His first miracle of turning water into wine, He sent the wine to the governor of the feast (John 2:8). He was demonstrating to us who minister in the new wine of the Holy Ghost that our new wine should be submitted to the one in charge. We need people in authority in our local church to test and judge our spiritual revelations. This is what the governor of the marriage feast at Cana represented prophetically. Pastors and leaders give a spiritual taste test, if you will. They are to judge the taste of the gift manifested and how it was presented to determine if it is in decency and order.

You may be thinking, "What if the pastor doesn't see my gift or receive my prophecy?" In learning boundaries and protocol in ministry, there is never a guarantee we will be handled correctly all the time, or even that we will be perfectly understood and received. That is par for the course. The key is that we follow whatever boundaries are there and trust that God will make room for us when He truly wants to use us to say something. Notice that Jesus didn't push for His opportunity; He just submitted what He had. He wasn't trying to prove He was a prophet or that He had any spiritual power. He just trusted that God would use Him and open the way to make it happen.

The church of Corinth wanted their spiritual moment of recognition while being indecent and out of order. Think about what it means to be indecent and out of order from the terms of Paul the apostle. When individuals are indecent and disorderly, they are loud, obnoxious, rude, fleshly, noncompliant to rules, inconsiderate of others, selfish, and often disrespectful to the authorities when they show up. They usually think there is a special set of rules that apply only to them. This is why they may be arrested, ticketed, or told to get in order.

Whether inside the church or not, we need orderly behavior when it comes to the things of the Spirit. We should be considerate and thoughtful, follow the rules, act in love, and honor others. This may mean there will be times you cannot share your "word" but trust that if it is truly from God, the Lord will make a way for it to be shared in the right way and in the right time and place. And if that right time never presents itself, then there will be times when you chalk it up to a learning experience in your ability to hear the Lord's secrets. Sometimes God will only share it with you for your own practice and growth, and it may never get shared.

There have been times in ministry when I was present in a service along with many different preachers who minister in the prophetic. At times, the one in charge would give an opportunity for any of us to share something we were hearing from the Lord. There have been many times I have felt something, but the open door to speak up didn't make its way to me. I just realize that there will be those times when I will have to keep what I am feeling to myself and accept the fact the God didn't have need of my "word" at that moment. Keeping that attitude is called following boundaries and having manners.

TAKE HEED TO YOURSELF

I want to address protocol boundaries for ministering to strangers. I certainly do not want to convey that we shouldn't share the Lord's secrets with those we don't know. We are sharing the gospel, and it is meant to touch the whole world!

But in this key area, we need to check ourselves, especially when it comes to the unsaved. Your moment of ministry to them may forever shape their view of the church, of Christians, and especially of those who minister in the things of the Spirit. We need to evaluate our motives and determine how the Lord wants us to minister to that person at that moment, rather than just try to seize our moment to shine.

A great example of how to minister to strangers is found in Exodus 19 and 24. God was going to come down and speak to His people, but He set up some guidelines that needed to be followed. He still does the same today when sharing His secrets.

Let's look at the boundaries and limitations that God established:

> You shall set bounds for the people all around, saying, "Take heed to yourselves that you do not go up to the mountain or touch its base. Whoever touches the mountain shall surely be put to death."
>
> —EXODUS 19:12

Let me draw your attention to the phrase that says, "Take heed to yourselves." In other words, examine yourself, keeping yourself in check. What if these people decided to ignore the boundaries and limits set by God and given to Moses? They would have died. What if they decided to be mavericks and lone rangers and storm the mountain because they felt the rules didn't apply to them? What if they thought Moses as their leader was just being controlling? Sadly, this is how some treat the prophetic. They want to establish their own guidelines, rules, and standards of ministering the things of God. They don't want to take heed to themselves, so they minister outside the church in a reckless way. They assume that any teaching or leader who wants to establish the prophetic or things of God with certain boundaries and limitations is just trying to control them.

On the other hand, it is also important for leaders to avoid putting excessive stipulations on the prophetic that stem more from their own frustrations. Doing this can push the operation of the prophetic completely out of the church. Some leaders carry a great deal of insecurity in the gifts of the Spirit and are even more insecure about their church members being used in them. If you feel your ability to minister in the prophetic will simply never grow in your current church, then you need to pray about whether that will be your church for the long haul. Otherwise, you run the risk of becoming offended with the church, and then you will get in trouble with God. You will have to come to terms with the fact that you will have to flow with that church and rejoice while doing it.

Good leaders do need to establish true proper guidelines that promote a healthy avenue for the people to be used in the prophetic, especially for those who are particularly geared that way. However, don't be pushy with your pastor. Give your leader time to develop the right avenues and programs for the prophetic to flourish. You can trust that he or she will do that, especially when that person has already exhibited a heart for people to prophesy or be used in the gifts. Like Moses, leaders are entrusted by God to properly facilitate boundaries and limitations that encourage God's voice, just as Moses did on the mountain.

So, if we intend to minister God's secrets to someone we don't know outside the church or to someone who is not saved, then how do we make sure we are "taking heed to ourselves" and doing it correctly? Here are some guidelines to help you:

1. *Make sure your ability to minister God's secrets has been proven inside the church first.* Before you step out to minister to others outside the church, especially the unsaved, you need to practice inside the church. Let your pastor and other appointed leaders see how you function. They need to see not only how you function in the gifts but also how you function as a Christian in general. You don't need a great deal of personal interaction with the pastor to accomplish this. You just need to live right, get involved in the church, get in the right place to grow prophetically, and then let God establish you. Believe me, your pastor and his or her leaders will eventually become aware of your commitment and ability and see your proven fruit.

2. *Make sure you are not ministering in a way that draws attention to yourself and away from Jesus.* Some people do strange things when they prophesy. All of us may have certain "-isms" when we minister, but we need to work hard to eliminate some of the most obvious ones. I make a point to work on these in my own life. That person outside the church (or even inside for that matter) may not be able to get past the weird way you shake your head or squint your eyes while you minister to them. To you it may feel powerful and anointed, but to others it may look odd. I once heard a minister say, "If you want to grow in how you deliver ministry to other people, record yourself on video and watch it. You will be surprised at what you see!" Certain habitual jerks, filler phrases, and facial expressions can distract people and draw attention to yourself. Getting too close to people's faces when you talk to them,

or shouting at them, can hinder people from receiving and can misrepresent you, especially to the unsaved person. I do not want to make you paranoid or so tight that you can't move a muscle when you prophesy. However, you want to get rid of overdramatized behavior.

3. *Make sure your habit is not to be "outside the church" and on your own all the time.* Certainly we should be able to minister the prophetic things of God on the street. This is biblical, and people in the Bible did minister outside the church service setting. However, that should never be your only venue for sharing God's secrets. Some people make a habit of grabbing opportunities at the back of churches, in parking lots, and in similar places to constantly share what they *receive.* I am not saying that you will never receive a word for someone as you carry on a conversation with that person. Let's face it, we *are* a prophetic people, and revelation can come at any moment in time. However, the problem arises if your normal intention is to make a place for yourself. With that intent, people end up getting hurt.

Here is the real clincher on it. Are you involved in prophetic experiences within the pastor's set boundaries, such as in a service when the opportunity is given or at prophetic training sessions or discipleship groups? Have you taken the time to learn from your church's established programs and protocols for the prophetic? If your answer is *no* and it is *always* outside of the radar of accountability in the parking lot after church that you prophesy, then you may be creating a problem by operating outside the boundaries God wants you to follow.

Jesus taught boundaries and limitations in Luke 10 by giving His disciples instruction before sending them out. He didn't discourage them from ministering in the power and gifts of God outside of His watchful eye. He just made sure they were accountable to Him and properly trained before they went. It wasn't until later, after following His teaching and example for three years, that they were given the opportunity to do more on their own.

Notice that Jesus followed up on them by going to the places they had gone. He was able to see if the fruit left behind them was beneficial or a detriment. Had they followed His boundaries and guidelines, Jesus would be able to see the fruit of their ministry when He arrived. Luke 10:1 says, "After these things the Lord appointed seventy others also, and sent them two by two before His face into every city and place where He Himself was about to go." These disciples were given parameters and were entrusted to minister accordingly, knowing that Jesus would come after and see the good their ministry accomplished.

Eli the priest trained the great prophet Samuel. Samuel ministered before his leader as he learned how to correctly hear and minister the things of God. "Then the boy Samuel ministered to the LORD before Eli" (1 Samuel 3:1). I have heard people say, "Well, I don't have a good pastor or a great church that I can learn from in the prophetic." This may be true, but many use this as a reason to be unaccountable and go about sharing the things of God without anyone to whom they are properly submitted. Some use this as an excuse because they don't want anyone putting proper boundaries and limitations on them. Others feel that no church or pastor is properly qualified to speak into their lives or understand the uniqueness of their gifts. So they become self-appointed intercessors, prophets, and ministers who operate like loose cannons, shooting whenever and wherever they want.

This is one of the reasons many pastors don't develop prophetic outlets for the members of their congregation. Because they have to control all the flakiness that goes with undisciplined people, rather than create any prophetic training, they shut it down altogether and keep all prophesying to that which they do or other pastors on their staff do. Sure, Eli was not a great example of a mentor by the choices he made in discipling his own sons. Yet, God still used him to train Samuel, and, as a result, God didn't allow Samuel's words to fall to the ground.

God can train you to share His secrets regardless of your leader and his or her style of leadership if you will give your heart to the vision of your church and be committed and accountable. It is imperative that you do not just go about sharing the secrets of God and speaking into people's lives *until you have received the proper input, guidance, and boundaries.*

In the church we pastor, we love to train the people to hear from God and give them opportunity to be used in the gifts. Then, after they have proven that they can properly represent Jesus, we look for ways to help them share the secrets of God to others in a proper and correct manner.

DIFFERENT LEVELS OF RESPONSIBILITY

Looking again at the example in Exodus 19 and 24 of Moses and the children of Israel at the mountain, we can see that not all the people were at the same level in their experience or delegated authority. Some had to remain at the bottom of the mountain while others were given passage to get a closer and deeper prophetic revelation. The higher they went up the mountain, the more they were able to get a glimpse of God, but greater responsibility and accountability were required of them also.

The boundaries and limitations established by God at each level were for the spiritual betterment of all involved. For example, a pastor may not have to follow the identical boundaries of his congregation, but there will be other boundaries by which he or she will need to abide that are not required of the congregation.

This principle is illustrated in the example of the river of God in Ezekiel 47. There were four different levels of the river to be measured. This river speaks of God's power and the different levels in which people minister, each requiring different boundaries and limitations. The river's levels were measured at the ankle, knee, waist, and a level that requires the person to swim. With each step, there was a new measurement in the river. This illustrates how we need to properly handle the things of God. We are to be submitted to proper authority to measure our steps and character as we go deeper. The more responsible we are, the greater depth and responsibility will be given.

The deeper you go in the flow of the river of God's power, the more disciplined, trained, skilled, and prepared you need to be. Just as in a natural river, the deeper you go, the faster the current. In the depths of God there is very little room for the flesh, or else one could drown. At each level, there is greater exposure to criticism, insecurity, and error. At the deepest level, mistakes and errors in how you minister become more detrimental and hurtful because they usually occur on a platform before many people who are looking to you as a sound source of leadership and direction in their lives.

There are some additional examples in Scripture that point to the reasons we need boundaries and limitations:

- Understanding that just because you prophesy or are a prophet does not mean you will operate as one in every setting is an important boundary—"Many widows were in Israel in the days of Elijah...but to none of them was Elijah sent except to Zarephath" (Luke 4:25–26).

- Acknowledging the Holy Spirit's different expressions holds us to boundaries—"There are diversities of gifts...differences of ministries...diversities of activities....But the manifestation of the Spirit is given to each one for the profit of all" (1 Corinthians 12:4–7).

- Doing things with love is a boundary—"Though I speak with the tongues of men and of angels, but have not love,

I have become sounding brass or a clanging cymbal" (1 Corinthians 13:1).

- Realizing we don't have all the revelation all the time is a boundary—"For we know in part and we prophesy in part" (1 Corinthians 13:9).

- Seeing the true purpose of prophecy is an example of a boundary—"But he who prophesies speaks edification and exhortation and comfort to men" (1 Corinthians 14:3).

- Appreciating that we need those who judge our prophetic ministry is a boundary—"Let two or three prophets speak, and let the others judge" (1 Corinthians 14:29).

- Order is a required boundary—"Let all things be done decently and in order" (1 Corinthians 14:40).

- Knowing that not all are gifted in certain areas is a boundary—"And He Himself gave some to be apostles, some prophets, some evangelists, and some pastors and teachers" (Ephesians 4:11).

PUTTING THE STONES IN ORDER

Sometimes we only focus on what happens when we don't follow proper boundaries, such as the case with Moses and the mountain. Yet, what can happen when we follow God's established boundaries and stay in certain guidelines? God's intent on the mountain was to manifest His power among the people. In fact, His real desire was that the people hear His voice—He wanted them to hear His secrets! That is still God's intention today. Let's study what good comes when we stay in the proper guidelines.

In 1 Kings 18, Elijah confronted the prophets of Baal on Mount

Carmel. From Scripture, we know that during that time in history, Israel's twelve tribes were divided, with ten of its tribes settling to the north and the other two making up the southern kingdom. Yet God didn't see His twelve tribes of Israel divided, which we see from the example of Elijah placing all twelve stones in order together and referring to them as "Israel." "And Elijah took twelve stones, according to the number of the tribes of the sons of Jacob, to whom the word of the LORD had come, saying, 'Israel shall be your name'" (1 Kings 18:31).

God still saw Israel as one nation. Elijah followed His instructions to set twelve stones in order, and, as a result, fire fell from heaven! As long as there was disorder and disunity, the fire and glory of God didn't fall. But once order came, the power of God manifested! Some people think that if you establish order, you will hinder the Holy Spirit from flowing. But an orderly place to move powerfully is just what the Holy Spirit needs.

This same principle of order was true when the mother of two of the twelve disciples wanted her sons to be granted special privileges. This angered the other ten disciples, which caused quite a storm (Matthew 20:20–24). This happens in the church today when competition, pride, and an air of superiority exist among its members. Some people seem most concerned about who gets to be seated in the places of importance, who gets the most recognition, and whose prophecy is the best. This causes division and keeps the fire of God from falling.

Initially, Jesus's disciples always seemed to be fighting for a prominent position, which created disorder among them. In fact, they even lost one disciple in the mayhem when Judas committed suicide after betraying Jesus. In the end, there were only eleven original apostles. It is important to remember that the number twelve in Scripture often speaks of God's kingdom order. As when God established order in a divided Israel through Elijah's altar of twelve stones, the kingdom was again out of order in God's eyes with just eleven apostles. It was not until they replaced Judas with Matthias and had all twelve apostles again that the fire of the Holy Spirit fell. The apostles represented the same stones that Elijah used in 1 Kings 18. In 1 Peter 2:5 we are told that we are living stones! When the stones are set in order—when the members of God's kingdom are in order—then and only then can the fire of God fall. That is when we will have God's power in manifestation, just as with Moses, Elijah, and the twelve apostles.

Another example is found in 2 Samuel 6. King David wanted to bring God's power and presence back to Jerusalem for all to benefit, but he neglected the proper order and guidelines for transporting the ark. Rather than bringing the ark of the covenant that housed His presence back on the shoulders of the priests, as God required, David decided to bring it back by setting it upon a cart drawn by an ox. This looked harmless and innocent enough, right? Not hardly! Suddenly the ox stumbled.

When a man named Uzzah reached out to keep it from falling, he died (2 Samuel 6:6–7). Why did this happen? The Bible says that because David didn't follow the Lord's order, depending instead on his own guidelines, his disobedience cost Uzzah his life: "For because you bore it not [as God directed] at the first, the Lord our God broke forth upon us—because we did not seek Him in the way He ordained" (1 Chronicles 15:13, AMP).

Of course, most of us know how the story turned out. This tragic event caused David to become angry with the Lord, and so he decided to remove the power of God to another place (2 Samuel 6:8). The power of God was meant to be a blessing, but when proper order was not followed, it had very harmful results. The same is true for the secrets of God. They are ordained of God and necessary today. They are meant to be a great blessing, but when used contrary to proper guidelines, they are often harmful, causing people to mistrust prophets or those who prophesy. This leads many leaders to become offended and hurt and distrustful of the prophetic, and they do just what David did when Uzzah died—they send it away.

David sent the ark of the covenant away to the house of Obed-Edom. He *put it on the shelf*, so to speak, and didn't want anything to do with it. David later realized that Obed-Edom's house was getting blessed by having the ark, which caused him to reestablish the correct order and to bring the presence of God back to Jerusalem. This time it became a blessing!

Let this example from the life of David encourage you. Rather than shutting down the prophetic and avoiding it because you feel too many people have been hurt by the misuse of the prophetic gift, make the choice to bring the presence of God and the prophetic back to your life and into the life of your church. When David established the proper order, the result for him was a blessing. The result today will be the presence of God and His voice working among us! When proper biblical and ethical guidelines are established, the people of God can experience healthy, powerful prophetic gifts in their lives and churches.

COME BY THE DOOR

Jesus reiterated the need for boundaries in John 10:1: "Most assuredly, I say to you, he who does not enter the sheepfold by the door, but climbs up some other way, the same is a thief and a robber." What does it mean to come by the way of the door in relation to decency, order, and boundaries in the prophetic? To come by the way of the door into the sheepfold is to follow the proper order established by the shepherd who oversees it, which we have been talking about in detail.

Most of the sheepfolds in the day of Jesus had only one door, and the only way in and out was to pass by the shepherd. In this way, the shepherd could more easily protect the sheep from outside harm, such as wolves. Anyone attempting to come in by some other way would be considered a thief and a robber according to this verse! In other words, there is a proper way to enter the sheepfold, or to enter the church. When people try to sneak in unaccounted for, they are considered to be thieves and robbers.

Thieves and robbers enter in by their own terms and methods. They usually want to remain disguised from the person in charge but seek to have access to the sheep. As I mentioned earlier, some so-called *prophets* go around giving prophetic words without allowing themselves or their words to be tested. They look for the precious things of the church to claim as theirs. They steal from the people and from the vision for that church. Thieves and robbers are usually undisciplined and unconcerned about using the door. They really don't care what the rules of the house are—they make up their own rules.

I have had to deal with people who have a thief and robber spirit in the church I pastor. A woman once stated that she was prophetic and wanted to prophesy to the congregation on her first Sunday in my church. When she arrived, she immediately asked one of our leaders where to sit up front so she could prophesy. She said that the Lord had told her that this was her church and I was her pastor.

I didn't even know this woman. However, it became clear to me that she had no intention of being a blessing. Though she was unproven, she wanted to pull people aside and give them a word without me knowing about it. She felt the need to prophesy and to send letters and e-mails filled with her *prophetic* point of view. This is the spirit of the thief and robber!

I finally had to confront her and tell her that her behavior was not appropriate. I explained that we do not let anyone just come and prophesy to the congregation or to individual people in the church without myself and our leadership knowing that person and before that person first gets plugged into the training we have established. If you are going to speak into the lives of the people God has called me to oversee, then I want to know a little bit about you. After all, as the shepherd, I am to take good care of God's sheep!

She didn't receive the guidelines I established and felt I didn't view her the way God did. Her need for attention and her disorderly behavior made this fact obvious. She even e-mailed corrective words to the church.

She dishonored the *door* of entry into our church and just wanted her own moment, stealing what belonged to another.

People like this woman become what Jesus said in Matthew 12:30: "He who is not with Me is against Me, and he who does not gather with Me scatters abroad." This verse describes how many pastors feel. Like Jesus, they need people who will help to build the vision and seek to promote unity—not those who fight for their own independence. As a pastor I can recognize those who do not come by the door. They do not desire to gather; instead, they scatter. They are not there to seek unity or help build the local church. Rather, they are out to do something separate, independent, and unaccounted for and to scatter others through self-promotion. Those who scatter are those who do things by their own set of rules. It is because of these people that others mistrust the prophetic.

We can see the example of Jesus in Matthew 23:37–38. He tried to gather and protect the people by sending them prophets, but the people did not receive them and killed them instead! "O Jerusalem, Jerusalem, the one who kills the prophets and stones those who are sent to her! How often I wanted to gather your children together, as a hen gathers her chicks under her wings, but you were not willing! See! Your house is left to you desolate."

Jesus was painting a picture of the safety that comes from the prophetic when it is experienced under the guidelines God sends and endorses. It is meant to offer a covering that gathers and promotes order and unity. But by rejecting it, the house of Israel became desolate. We face the same result when we don't promote proper prophetic order and boundaries. People can become confused and wounded. Leaders and churches will become void of the prophetic without established order and safety. Misuse scatters and kills the prophetic things of God.

How can we promote the right prophetic order in our lives and churches? If you are a leader, you should create a safe sheepfold that establishes biblical gifts of the Spirit with awesome results. If you are a church member, you should seek to promote the good of the kingdom over your own agenda. Here are some additional things that both the leader and the people can do to help the prophetic flow correctly.

Do all things in love

The Bible tells us to do all things in love. Love promotes others over self. It promotes unity. Love is always the most important principle in ministering the secrets of God. The apostle Paul said that if we had the gifts of the Spirit operating in our lives but didn't do it in love, we were just making a noise like a loud cymbal (1 Corinthians 13:1).

Learning and teaching people to walk in love will help promote order. Love is clearly defined in 1 Corinthians 13:4–8. The Amplified Version gives a very detailed account of these powerful verses:

> Love endures long and is patient and kind; love never is envious nor boils over with jealousy, is not boastful or vainglorious, does not display itself haughtily. It is not conceited (arrogant and inflated with pride); it is not rude (unmannerly) and does not act unbecomingly. Love (God's love in us) does not insist on its own rights or its own way, for it is not self-seeking; it is not touchy or fretful or resentful; it takes no account of the evil done to it [it pays no attention to a suffered wrong]. It does not rejoice at injustice and unrighteousness, but rejoices when right and truth prevail. Love bears up under anything and everything that comes, is ever ready to believe the best of every person, its hopes are fadeless under all circumstances, and it endures everything [without weakening]. Love never fails [never fades out or becomes obsolete or comes to an end]. As for prophecy (the gift of interpreting the divine will and purpose), it will be fulfilled and pass away; as for tongues, they will

be destroyed and cease; as for knowledge, it will pass away [it will lose its value and be superseded by truth].

If we would apply this definition to the prophetic secrets and how we minister them, it would create a healthier respect for the prophetic. It would help us to prophesy in a way that is patient and kind. It would train us when it comes to the prophetic not to be envious, jealous, and boastful of other people. When we deliver a prophetic secret, we shouldn't display ourselves arrogantly or unmannerly. When we desire to minister the secrets of God in love, we would not insist on our own way and rights, being self-seeking, resentful, or touchy. Imagine what would happen if we who want to minister in the secrets of God would practice this. Or what if we as leaders made this a standard to all who covet to prophesy? I believe the secrets of God would manifest in decency and order.

Discipline

Discipline comes by being led by the Holy Spirit, checking our motives, and being submitted to proper authority. It is also important that we are willing to stay within certain guidelines, even when they don't mesh with our preference at the time. Discipline and growth go together. Children need discipline and training to make them well-rounded adults. The same is true for those growing in the prophetic. Depending upon the child's age and behavior, different disciplinary measures and boundaries are given. The same is true for those who are in different places or situations in the prophetic. Sometimes it is a quiet time and a time-out. In other words, there may be no freedom to prophesy until a person matures and the leader feels that person's behavior is proven. At other times, a different discipline may be necessary. While people in our churches are not natural children, and I am not suggesting that leaders treat them as such, it is still crucial that they learn the biblical principles of discipline.

To enter by the door and operate correctly, we must be open to the growing process, which may require loving, proper discipline to guide the maturity process. Discipline brings proper training in love.

Equipping

There are many who want to come into the door of a church and learn to effectively minister the secrets of God. They want to do what is right but have no one to equip or train them. As leaders, we must give the tools, teachings, principles, and opportunities for people to learn, grow, and succeed in ministering the secrets of God. We can't speak negatively of those who do not handle the prophetic well when we do little to equip them. It is important, as well, for those who want to learn to hear and minister the secrets of God to be equipped. Keep in mind that equipping can be different in every church. Just because you were trained a certain way in one church does not mean the next pastor will receive you the same way. Never stop being willing to grow and learn wherever you are.

The process of training may seem frightening and intimidating for those who want to be trained. This is why it is best to provide the safety of special classes to equip people. Prophetic training sessions, discipleship groups, and classes give people a smaller setting and make them feel less nervous about making a mistake. It is better to make mistakes in prophesying among a few who are learning along with you than before a crowd!

Small groups also allow the opportunity to affirm and value those who are trying and want to learn to prophesy correctly. Tell them they are doing a good job when doing so. Let them know when you feel they are truly hearing from the Lord. This is encouraging to those whom we expect to follow proper protocol and accountability. Don't focus only on the mistakes, but also focus on the good. Encourage them to keep stepping out. Leaders must make the boundaries and guidelines clear for those who are growing in their gifting.

The Voice of Strangers

There is another important concept in John 10, where Jesus was talking about the sheepfold.

> And when he brings out his own sheep, he goes before them; and the sheep follow him, for they know his voice. Yet they will by no means follow a stranger, but will flee from him, for they do not know the voice of strangers.
>
> —John 10:4-5

For some reason, people have a tendency to listen to people who are unproven in spiritual things over those in their lives who have been proven to be worthy of trust. Some people would rather listen to the input, sermon, or prophecy of a complete stranger over those they have known for years. For example, they choose to believe the opinion of some Internet ministry they don't know personally over the voice of their pastor for the last ten years. I believe this tendency is due mostly to the problem in human nature of becoming familiar and bored with what is before us every day. We become starstruck and mesmerized by the new and spectacular.

I am not implying that we can't prophesy to or receive a prophesy from someone we don't know. But we just need to be wise with what we receive from those we don't know. We tell our children to beware of strangers. This is not done because of suspicion or a desire to control but, rather, in order to provide guidelines and promote boundaries with our children that keep them safe. This is true for leaders who want to train people in the prophetic. It is unwise to follow the flattering words of a stranger over a trusted leader to whom you are submitted.

I have seen this happen in the lives of some of the people in my church. For example, years ago a couple in my church wanted to get married, but I felt uneasy about it in my heart. After seeking the Lord about it, I was convinced they shouldn't get married, and I told them I could not perform their ceremony. They didn't listen to my counsel and took the advice of a friend who insisted that I was wrong about them. The friend advised the couple to get married, which they did before the justice of the peace. Their marriage only lasted a short time, and they later divorced. Had they listened to their pastor over this stranger, they would not have married.

On another occasion, a visitor came to the midweek service at our church and suddenly interrupted me at the end of service in order to give a prophecy. I don't normally allow visitors to prophesy, much less interrupt me in the pulpit, but I could tell the person was not from this country and had a heavy accent. I was gracious to her, realizing she did not know our normal guidelines.

Initially, I was going to stop her, but the word seemed accurate and bore witness in my heart that it could be from the Lord. I just dismissed the fact that this person did not understand our protocol. I chose to listen to the word and heard things that seemed to be coming from the Lord. After the service, I met the visitor and let her know I was encouraged by the word and so were the people.

However, I also politely let her know she didn't have to interrupt the service, and I explained how we do things in our church. I let her know we encouraged the prophetic but with certain healthy guidelines. This person continued to come back during the midweek services and still tried to do the same thing. She completely ignored what I clearly told her about guidelines in our church.

I let her prophesy a second time, which was entirely out of character for me. But again, since she was from another country, I thought perhaps she didn't understand me the first time. Besides, the first time her word was powerful and blessed me.

The third week she tried to interrupt me at the end of the service, I'd had enough. I told this person right from the pulpit that she needed to stop interrupting me at the end of services and needed to get under proper pastoral authority. I let her know she was not to prophesy in our church again until she was submitted here. I normally don't like to correct someone publicly, but she gave me no choice. We never saw this stranger again.

I believe she had a legitimate gift but had not been properly taught and was unwilling to be taught. She never learned how to enter into the door and honor the one in authority. It was obvious she was not here for my church's benefit but only for herself and her gift. She wanted me to forgo years of hard labor, prayer, and fasting for her three prophetic words.

The problem is that too often people start out right with a word that seems accurate and then end up wrong by wanting to be the center of attention. The pastor is left to clean up the mess or try to explain the truth to the sheep when something wrong gets said.

On one occasion, just as my family and I were sitting down at home to eat, a stranger walked into our home unannounced. We felt that a stranger who assertively entered without knocking or being invited had violated the order of our home. In the case of this stranger, it was an accident. He was visiting a friend who had told him on the phone to come in when he arrived, but he accidentally had the wrong home! However, when it first happened, I reacted defensively and was immediately ready for a confrontation.

That is what strangers do to pastors and the people when they enter a church house in the same imposing manner. People feel uneasy simply because they don't know them or their agenda. No one likes to feel violated, imposed upon, or made uncomfortable by someone they don't know. We have to make sure we don't barge into churches and people's lives as this stranger did. Remember, we are to enter by the door. We need to win trust and be proven in the church no matter what area of the ministry we get involved in.

Even Jesus stood at the door and knocked in the Book of Revelation. He didn't barge His way into the door of our hearts (Revelation 3:20).

Do you know that Nathan the prophet entered by the door when he came to speak to David the king? When David committed adultery with Bathsheba and then had her husband killed and tried to cover it up, the prophet did not run in before the king, screaming out a confrontation. He knew his boundaries and limitations with the secrets of God. In fact, Nathan was not a stranger to David. He was a proven, trusted prophet David knew. He was not just some random prophet who decided to stop in on David in the court. I don't believe God uses random individuals to send corrective or admonishing words to pastors, leaders, and those in a place of authority. If God is going to speak this type of admonishment to you, it will be through those who are proven in ministry and/or proven in your own life! I don't put stock in prophecies from people I have never heard of and that come via e-mail, mail, or other methods, especially if the words are a rebuke. This is disrespectful and out of order.

Nathan approached David as a gentleman. He didn't come intrusively or unmannerly. He knew his boundaries and limitations with those in authority. He didn't sweep the sin under the rug, but with great wisdom, respect, and honor, he gave his prophetic word about David's sin in the form of a story.

We can learn from him how to treat those in authority in our lives. We shouldn't go up to the pastor, or anyone else for that matter, with out-of-order methods. Nor should we barge into churches and expect to be given the right to give a directive voice to that church. We are not in the business of prophesying in order to expose people's sins, pronounce judgment against them, or condemn them. This type of behavior is indecent and disorderly. When Nathan, a trusted prophet of the day, came in, sent by God with respect, he not only honored David, but he also honored God.

Another example of this is found in the house of Jesse, David's father. Samuel the prophet asked Jesse if all his children were present for him to prophesy to them: "And Samuel said to Jesse, 'Are all the young men here?' Then he said, 'There remains yet the youngest, and there he is, keeping the sheep.' And Samuel said to Jesse, 'Send and bring him. For we will not sit down till he comes here'" (1 Samuel 16:11). The word from the Lord was for him to go to the house of Jesse. Samuel obeyed that, but he went respectfully through Jesse, the father of the house, before ministering to his sons. He used boundaries and limitations. Samuel didn't come in as a stranger and act like a thief and a robber. For him to prophesy, Jesse had to give Samuel the liberty to do so.

If we desire to share the secrets of the Lord, we must be like Samuel and Nathan the prophets. We must honor another man's kingdom and house. This will take us from being a stranger who carries the spirit of the thief and robber, to a chosen, trusted, honorable vessel for the Lord to use. You will gain the honor of God and the honor of those you will minister to.

ROOSTERS, DONKEYS, AND WHALES

As we bring this chapter on boundaries and limitations in the prophetic to a close, I want to give you some brief teaching on how God will set back in order those who refuse. It is evident from Scripture that if people refuse to listen to the instructions of God or their leaders, the Lord will use other things to bring them back to order, boundaries, limitations, and obedience. In the Bible, God used the mouths of a donkey, rooster, and whale to speak prophetically to those who needed to be set back in order. It sounds funny, but it's true!

God used literal animals in the Bible, but these examples hold a prophetic picture for us today.

The rooster—Matthew 26

Jesus told Peter that after Peter denied Him three times, a rooster would crow. The sound from this rooster was a reminder to Peter of what Jesus prophesied earlier. Once he heard it, he had to ask himself, "Am I for Jesus's kingdom, or am I going to deny it, being given the opportunity?" God will do this same thing today by using our leaders to help us correctly in the prophetic things of God. The example of the rooster's crowing wakes us up to our motives and intentions.

God will use certain situations, like a rooster's crowing, to test your heart's motive. Are you ready for the vision of God in the church you attend? Or, if given the opportunity, would you deny the vision to promote your own agenda? People will often say casually, "I love the vision of this church, and I love you, Pastor." But it may be different once their hearts have been tested. Today, an example of a rooster's crowing might be when the pastor asks you to take a season away from prophesying or ministering until you get some training, repositioning, and development in some area of your life. Everything inside you wants to disagree with his point of view because you feel you are called to speak! Can you hear the rooster crowing? These rooster crows are meant to test your heart and motives.

The donkey—Numbers 22

Balaam was the prophet of God who kept giving the secrets of the Lord into the enemy's hand. He was using the prophetic things of God for his own personal gain, compromise, and even betrayal of God's people, and it made God angry. So God opened the mouth of a donkey to speak to the prophet Balaam. As the story goes, his donkey had seen an angel that kept standing in the donkey's way, forcing the donkey to give this unruly prophet a rough ride! Initially, Balaam didn't see the angel and became angry with the donkey. He struck her three times with a rod. Finally, the donkey spoke up and told Balaam that what he was doing was wrong. Prophetically, the Lord was using the donkey to hinder the prophet's compromising actions and set this prophet in order.

Of course, we know that donkeys are also a symbol of stubbornness, religion, and rebellion. When we become stubborn, God will get in our way and hinder our actions. We hear the donkey speak when we are on a certain course, and we know we need to make changes, but we refuse. We want to do what we want and like to do, and we reason that it is

God's will for us. For example, people hear the teaching about the need for prophetic training and the need to get plugged into the right church, but still they refuse. They reason why that type of boundary will not work for them. Usually there are certain sins in the mix that they don't want to deal with.

When you hear messages that challenge you to change, respond to them. Otherwise, you will keep feeling hindered in your gift and find yourself unable to be used the way God intended for you to be used. God *will* hinder your path when it is pointed toward compromise. Don't get stubborn and angry and strike back the way Balaam did. Be teachable and willing to change. The donkey's mouth is meant to get us back on course. When we are obedient, we can be trusted to handle the secrets of the Lord honorably.

The whale—the Book of Jonah

Jonah, a prophet of the Lord, was instructed to go to Nineveh and tell the people in that city to repent because in forty days they would be judged. At first, Jonah refused to obey the Lord. Jonah ran to a city called Tarshish, known for its commerce and wealth. Jonah ran to where it was comfortable and easy. To his surprise, God had a whale waiting to swallow him before he ever made it to his vacation destination! Some people want the prophetic secrets of the Lord too easily. They want to be used by God as long as it doesn't require too much sacrifice. Others want to be used by God and will only follow shortcuts to get there. They want to prophesy, but they don't want to give the time to prayer, training, teaching, and study. They also don't want any type of commitment. They want to go into churches, blow in, blow up, and blow out. In other words, they come in, they prophesy, and they move on to the next free-and-easy platform.

God forced Jonah to do the very thing he didn't want to do. When he tried to avoid it, God sent a whale to swallow him. I am sure there was nothing easy or enjoyable about spending three days in a whale's stomach. Talk about discomfort and inconvenience! That probably made going to Nineveh look like a cakewalk indeed. Sometimes we make it harder on ourselves than the sacrifice God asked of us would have been after all. Prophetically the Lord uses the mouth of the whale to speak to us. You will find yourself in the whale's mouth going nowhere when you keep avoiding the sacrifices God asks you to make. You will keep revisiting the same issues until you break down and do what God wants.

That is why some people go from church to church, and the same problems and issues follow them each place they go. They want to avoid the sacrifice God wants them to make, and they get mad at the last pastor for addressing it, but it's still there. Until they make the sacrifice needed, they will never step into what God has for their lives. Ask yourself this question: Do I want to live a life of ease and comfort, loving the things of the world yet disobeying God? Many today would rather disobey and live in the comfort of Tarshish than be trained and equipped to transform lives and cities as God wanted Jonah to do in Nineveh.

WHAT GOD WANTS

Boundaries and limitations aren't meant to stifle, hinder, manipulate, and place unnecessary rules and stipulations on the prophetic. God wants to bring proper order into your life, which will allow God's power to flow through you and allow you to be a blessing to others.

We know that God is speaking today. He wants to speak to us. You can hear His voice and even share His secrets. When you apply the principles of this chapter, you will see that there is a benefit to proper order. It actually increases the manifestation of God's power. Be encouraged today to go ahead and minister the gospel. Seek to hear His voice and to learn the proper guidelines, and you will be a more prepared vessel, ready to hear and share the secrets of the Lord.

SIX

FALSE PROPHETS AND PROPHECIES, AND PROPHETIC MISTAKES

Now our knowledge is partial and incomplete, and even
the gift of prophecy reveals only part of the whole picture!
—1 Corinthians 13:9, NLT

H E IS PULLING OUT OF THE RACE!" THE WORDS STUNNED ME as I sat staring at the television set. The candidate I prophesied would become president was pulling out of the race.

"How could I have been wrong?" I questioned. The Lord had used me countless times to prophesy accurately about many elections from various nations, and now it appeared I made a serious error.

I had no personal interest in this candidate about whom I prophesied. I work hard to prophesy what I believe God is saying, and I realize that what God is saying is not always what the Lord wants to happen. So, in this case, I didn't feel I missed it because I wrongly prophesied out of a personal desire for this candidate to be elected. Prophets have to prophesy the facts that will come to pass, whether they represent their own preferences or not.

I had met personally with this candidate and shared what I had believed to be the word of the Lord for him. While I didn't generally say his name from the platform while prophesying, I had strongly hinted on many national platforms that I felt he was the one who would win. On other occasions, I privately shared with people who I felt the next president was going to be. Now I was facing a barrage of questions, both from others and from myself. Had I been too overconfident? Would this candidate run again? How would this word from God play out? Was it meant for another time? Did I flatly miss it? All these questions were going on in my heart because I always want to represent Jesus well and do the right thing. I immediately called my pastor, certain other national leaders, as well as the leaders in my own church. I wanted to let them know it appeared I had missed it and was willing to humble myself if I needed to.

I knew that those who love me most—my family and church members—are always more understanding. I also knew that there are always those in the world who want to stone you when you are wrong! And yes, I had some who used those oh-so-awful words that we in the prophetic hate to hear: "You are a false prophet!" Nobody wants to hear that, but it will probably be said about every prophet at one point or another, whether they missed or not.

People who believe that one failed prophecy equals a false prophet often imply that. This kind of rhetoric has gone on for years regarding the prophetic things of God. However, this is not true concerning prophets or prophecy today. Let me emphasize: *one wrong prophecy does not make you a false prophet.* As we will discover later in this chapter, this idea is not only unscriptural, but it has also kept many good-intentioned people from stepping out to share the secrets of the Lord correctly.

In the Bible, many of God's prophets were stoned unjustly because their prophecies appeared wrong or didn't seem to come to pass in the way expected. Others were stoned or put to death because the people hearing them simply refused to receive them as words from the Lord.

Under the kind of scrutiny that comes with the prophetic today, it would be easy to want to throw in the towel and stop sharing prophetic secrets. This is exactly what the devil wants! I am not implying that we can just prophesy any old thing without accountability and hope it comes to pass, but many people are too quick to point the finger and make rash judgments. There are many waiting in the shadows to scream *heresy* and *false prophecy* whenever a word doesn't seem to come to pass the way they think it should. They are waiting to pick up a stone of accusation to discredit good, honest ministers and the prophetic ministry. We should not be so quick to discredit those who prophesy, especially if they have proven Christlike character and the fruit of a proven track record.

We simply cannot label someone a false prophet based on whether his prophecies are accurate. To begin with, do you know that the Bible reveals some false prophets who actually had prophecies come to pass? Yes! False prophets can—and do—prophesy accurately! Whether a prophecy comes to pass or not is our primary measuring stick. It is not the primary way to judge the legitimacy of a prophet, and I will give you many biblical examples to show that this is true.

Sometimes people just want to accuse or stone prophets simply because they don't like what the prophet had to say, and for this reason, they quickly brand that prophet as false. Jesus mentioned this fact in Matthew 23:34, 37: "Therefore, indeed, I send you prophets, wise men, and scribes: some of them you will kill and crucify...O Jerusalem, Jerusalem, the one who kills the prophets and stones those who are sent to her!" They stoned God's spokesman unjustly. Unfortunately, this hasn't changed today. Many of God's servants are unjustly written about, talked about, and lied about in a modern-day stoning, so to speak.

In fact, even Jesus was accused of being a false prophet. How crazy is that? Many wanted to stone Jesus because of things He did, and He absolutely prophesied correctly! His words were true and His lifestyle honorable to God, yet the people thought He was false. Notice some of the things they falsely accused Jesus of doing:

- They said His miracles were false and of the devil (Matthew 12:24).

- People complained about His teachings and didn't agree with them (John 6:61).

- His own brothers thought He was a madman and didn't believe Him (John 7:5).

- They tried to stone Jesus in Judea (John 11).

Have you ever wondered why they blindfolded Jesus at the trial leading to His crucifixion? It was because they were accusing Him of being a false prophet and were mocking Him. "Now the men who held Jesus mocked Him and beat Him. And having blindfolded Him, they struck Him on the face and asked Him, saying, 'Prophesy! Who is the one who struck You?'" (Luke 22:63–64). They were saying, "If You were a true prophet, You would be able to tell who is hitting You while You are blindfolded!"

The truth of the matter is that if people were willing to falsely accuse Jesus in such a manner as this, then you can be sure they will do it to God's prophets today. The difference was that Jesus never made a mistake, and yet He was still falsely accused. He was threatened with stoning, and many times His enemies tried to kill Him.

So where does that leave us who are subject to human error and desire to be used by God to share His secrets? The thought could send shivers up and down your spine and make you want to run in terror for sure! Let's delve into this subject, and perhaps we can gain some reassurance.

WE KNOW IN PART AND PROPHESY IN PART

There are many reasons why prophecies may not come to pass. Sometimes it is because we prophesy erroneously. Even though we have a high standard for accuracy, some of our beloved standards and expectations are man-made, not biblical. I want to give you a closer look at them.

We begin by realizing that none of us knows everything. In fact, the Bible says, "We see in a mirror, dimly" (1 Corinthians 13:12). A couple verses earlier, it says, "Now our knowledge is partial and incomplete, and even the gift of prophecy reveals only part of the whole picture" (verse 9, NLT). In other words, there is not one person alive who knows everything when he or she prophesies or shares the word of the Lord. I believe this is the reason prophets hung out together in the Bible. They were known as "a company of prophets" in 1 Samuel 10:5 (KJV). When they spent time together around the things of God, the prophetic picture, or what the Lord was saying, became more complete. On their own, each had only a portion of the picture. It is like a puzzle with many separate pieces. It isn't until you put the pieces together that you can understand the picture clearly.

We see that prophets don't know everything from the example of Samuel when he went to the house of Jesse to anoint the next king of Israel. He was a very accurate prophet, but he initially started to anoint Eliab as the next king (1 Samuel 16:6–7), and the Lord had to interrupt him. Samuel started to anoint the wrong one! Even after that, Samuel still didn't have the whole picture about David. He didn't prophesy and say, "There is one who is not in this room, and his name is David; bring him in!" All he knew was that when Jesse brought his other seven sons before him, something didn't register with him about any of them. That was all of the picture he had up to that point. He had to ask a question to get more clarity: "Are all the young men here?" (1 Samuel 16:11). This reveals the human side of us through which every prophetic secret has to flow.

How about the prophet Elisha who ministered to the Shunammite woman? When she came to him grieved, he didn't initially know that her son had died. So he asked her, "Is it well with you? Is it well with your husband? Is it well with the child?" (2 Kings 4:26). He asked those questions because he didn't know what was wrong with her. This prophet was no different from you and me, and he needed to get further clarity.

As people, we know in part and prophesy in part. It is because of this factor that we can make potential mistakes, because we only see our part, or we don't yet have all the revelation of what God might be saying. This is why it is wise not to scream *false* when it appears a word hasn't come to pass. It is possible that the human vessel made an error on the timing, missed an important part of the word, or even unintentionally put his or her spin on it. We also have to be careful that we give ample time for the word to actually come to pass before we automatically assume it was false or that the one giving it was in error. Rest assured, we will make mistakes in our walk with God and, at times, even in the gifts of the Spirit.

So, then, you may be asking, "How can I trust any prophecy if it is always subject to mistakes?" As you read on, I think there will be some nuggets to help you answer that question in your own heart.

Sometimes the reason we only see a certain part is because the Lord knows that part is all our faith could handle. "Having then gifts differing according to the grace that is given to us, let us use them: if prophecy, let us prophesy in proportion to our faith" (Romans 12:6). God will often give you only a word that matches your level of faith.

I remember a time when I prophesied something that appeared to be a wrong prophecy. Later, I discovered that I was just seeing a fractional part. I was driving home from a church service with a friend who was starting a church in another city. He asked if I would pray with him about finding a place for his newly formed church to meet. I said sure, but I wasn't seeking a prophetic word for him; I was just planning to pray. As I pulled into my driveway, still praying, suddenly the Lord gave me a vision. I saw a building and the name of the street it was on. I saw other landmarks in addition to that, things like a name of a local food chain and a school. Then I heard the name of a person called Terry.*

---

* Not his real name

I asked my friend, "Do you know anyone by the name of Terry?" He said no.

Now, keep in mind that I had never been to the city where my friend was starting his church. He wrote down what I saw and heard. He didn't know where this place was or who Terry was, and he was not familiar with the name of the street I mentioned. When he got back home, he decided to try to find the street I named and the landmarks I saw. Well, he found the name of the street and even saw the landmarks, but there was no building there. "Hmm," I thought. "How could I see all the other details and there not be a building?"

So my friend found a building elsewhere to start his church. A few short years went by, and my friend's church was starting to grow out of their current meeting place. He decided to go out looking again and remembered the word I gave him. He drove back to the same location, and this time there was a new vacant building with a sign on it! He quickly realized that this building had actually been there in the prophetic future vision I saw, but when he drove by a few years earlier, there had been only vacant land. The building had not yet been built the first time he went. To top it off, he discovered that the owner of the building was a man named Mr. Terry. It was the same name that was mentioned in the prophecy earlier. His church meets in this building today.

This is a good example of why it is so important that we are not too quick to pick up stones or assume false or wrong prophecy. What if my friend had just decided once and for all that I made a mistake? He could have missed a tremendous blessing. However, I only saw a part of the picture. I didn't see the part about the building being built later. From what I could tell, the building was already there. It was not a wrong or false prophecy, as it may have appeared. It just had to play out in God's timetable. Human error could have easily aborted the blessing, either by my inability to see the whole picture or by my friend just assuming I had a vision that stemmed from a case of indigestion!

Human error can play into the prophetic in three primary ways:

1. *Wrong prophecy*—The one who is prophesying makes a mistake or doesn't correctly relay the word.

2. *Wrong choices*—Those hearing or receiving the word make choices or mistakes that hinder the word from coming to pass.

3. *Wrong interpretation*—Those either giving or hearing the word put their own interpretation on it, which was not what God wanted to communicate.

WRONG PROPHECY

Humans can and do make mistakes when ministering in the things of God. Because of the human-error factor, in the New Testament, God put in place a method for us to judge prophecy. Notice I said *judge the prophecy*, not the prophet. There is a different biblical method for judging a true or false prophet.

Right now I just want to focus on prophecy itself. Paul says that if prophets were prophesying in the church, other prophets were to judge their prophecies (1 Corinthians 14:29). No order was given to criticize them or to stone or discipline them if they prophesied wrong. Instead, the other prophets were to judge the word itself for accuracy and soundness.

The judging here wasn't to be done just for the wider public to send letters of criticism when they didn't agree with the prophecy. It was simply that the other prophets were to judge their words. Why is this factor so important? It is because prophets understand the office and gifting of the prophet. They carry prophetic insight and revelation that gives them the ability to *read into* the words of the prophecy in a way others may not do. This doesn't mean that they are the only ones who can correctly judge and discern prophetic secrets. It means they may have a better understanding and ability to do so because of the grace given to them and the way they have learned to view the prophetic.

Good prophets are willing to submit their words to other prophets for review. I have the prophecies I receive transcribed, and then I make sure other prophets I trust read them and give me feedback.

As Christians we can certainly judge the prophetic words we hear to make sure they fall in line with the spirit of Bible doctrine, and we should make sure of that. As Christians, any words we hear—whether prophetic, teaching, or preaching—should be judged against the Word of God.

We can also judge prophecy against our own spirits. The prophetic word should have an element that moves you in a positive way. That doesn't mean you will always like what was said in the prophecy, especially if it convicted you or stepped on your toes. However, the prophecy should either bless you or drive you to prayer. A prophecy that is from the Lord will drive you to God. Wrong or false prophecies will give you an uncertain feeling.

If you are unsure if a word is right but you think it might be right, keep the prophecy handy in the back of your mind until a future time. As God unfolds it, time will usually tell if the word was right on. It is easier to judge a prophecy when you are grounded by the foundation of a good Bible-based church that receives prophecy today. A good pastor and church provides a constant meal of good doctrine, which prepares you with the proper skills.

If a proven and trusted minister or person does make a mistake, you can be confident that the word will not be detrimental to you under these guidelines for judging prophecy. Let me reiterate: don't stone that person who prophesied when he or she makes an honest mistake.

There is a great illustration in 2 Kings 4:38–44. The prophet Elisha was meeting with his spiritual sons, who were being mentored by him in the prophetic. They were sitting down for a meal when the servant who was in charge of preparing the meal unintentionally put a poisonous gourd in the pot of stew. The sons of the prophets discerned that there was poison in the pot—not by human knowledge but by revelation knowledge from God—and it, thankfully, saved their lives. The servant who prepared the meal did not poison the stew on purpose. He wasn't trying to kill them; he made an honest human mistake. That fact, in and of itself, has prophetic significance. It means humans make mistakes! The others began to cry out to their mentor Elisha that there was poison in the stew!

The Bible records that Elisha then put some meal cake in the stew, which destroyed the poison and made it safe for everyone to eat. What can we learn from this story, and how does it apply to human mistakes in the prophetic? The fact that this happened in the context of Elisha mentoring his prophetic spiritual sons reveals the human need to grow in our gifts. In a nutshell, here are the things we can glean from this story when it comes to right and wrong prophecy:

1. We may make human mistakes like this servant who was trying his best to serve. Sure, his mistake could have affected others negatively, but God made sure that no one was harmed in the end.

2. It is important to stay close to a good mentor or pastor who is mature in the prophetic and in spiritual things. This is one reason why this story was written, showing Elisha the mentor in the presence of his prophetic protégés. A seasoned, mature minister will know what to do when we miss it, just like when the servant missed it. Elisha was there to help save their lives and their future prophetic ministries. Pastors and leaders will help to keep our prophetic gifting alive and undefiled. They will offer accountability and help should we need it, and they will help us to keep our gifts pure and poison free. Without this kind of proper leadership, there could be serious negative results.

3. The meal cake in the pot points us to the Word of God. Some want to operate in the secrets of God without being

grounded in the Word of God, and eventually this will cause us to become poisoned. It also reveals that every prophetic secret and action needs to line up with the bread of God's Word.

4. This mistake was not intentional or purposeful. False prophets *intend* to lead people astray. This should encourage us who want to grow in the prophetic things of God; sometimes we may miss it, thinking we have heard from God. However, to continue without the proper teaching and accountability of an *Elisha* or mentor who is a mature leader could be a matter of life or death.

5. In this story of Elisha, we can see that even though death was in the pot, there was grace! Grace was given in this human error, which took a potentially bad situation and made it right. There is also grace for us who are true servants of Christ in the New Testament and who want to minister the secrets of God and bring honor to Him.

Be encouraged. Sometimes prophecies will be spoken in error, but that doesn't mean you can no longer trust the prophetic. If you apply these principles for handling them rightly, when a correct prophecy comes your way, it will produce a great blessing in your life.

WRONG CHOICES

Sometimes prophecies don't appear to come to pass because of the wrong choices of those who heard or received the prophecy. Our bad choices can change our destiny, even if God intended something else for us. Wrong choices can abort a prophecy. Moses made a bad decision that compromised his destiny. Moses was supposed to lead the people not only out of Egypt but also into the land of promise. However, he struck the rock rather than speaking to it as God commanded him:

> Then Moses lifted his hand and hit the rock twice with his stick. Water began pouring out, and the people and their animals drank it. But the LORD said to Moses and Aaron, "Because you did not believe me, and because you did not honor me as holy before the people, you will not lead them into the land I will give them."
>
> —NUMBERS 20:11–12, NCV

This costly decision caused Moses to abort a portion of his destiny. Moses's moment of anger caused him to miss out on God's best. He ignored the instructions and guidelines given to him. Sometimes what God speaks or plans prophetically doesn't come to pass because of the choices people make. Many times people can receive a prophetic word, but because their decisions do not line up with and support the word prophesied, the prophecy is aborted.

When we do something different from what God says, responding in the flesh, the operation of the prophetic can be affected in a negative way. Even nations can abort the word of the Lord when they don't obey what God speaks. This happened with the nation of Israel. God prophesied many times through His prophets what His plan was for Israel. It was a prophetic plan of blessing, but because of the people's choices, the words prophesied were cut off.

This holds true for us personally as well. When we receive a prophecy, we need to line up our habits, our choices, and our plans to help bring that prophetic word into manifestation. If we don't, we run the risk of aborting the prophecy. It does not mean the prophecy was not accurate. It means that we didn't come into obedience to the prophecy and, thus, caused it to be aborted.

WRONG INTERPRETATION

Another reason prophecies do not seem to come to pass is simply because we didn't understand them or we interpreted them wrongly. Sometimes we add to the prophecy without realizing it. I think that is why Revelation 22:18–19 warns us against either adding to God's prophetic word or taking anything away from it. Sometimes we do that by only hearing from the prophecy the thing or things we like or want to hear. In other words, we like the part that tells us we are going to prosper and be blessed, but we don't like hearing words that admonish us to change. In that instance, it is easy to put our own spin on the prophecy!

Sometimes when we hear a word, we simply don't listen carefully, and thus we only hear a portion of what was said. Then we run the risk of mishandling it because we only respond to one part of it. For example, God may prophesy that He is going to bless us if we will pray diligently. We may only hear His plan to bless us, but if we fail to tune into the part about praying, we may end up not praying about it and then wonder where His blessing went. It would be easy to assume the prophecy was wrong when in fact it probably was right.

Misinterpreting the prophecy has caused many people to wrongly assume that a prophecy didn't come to pass. Sometimes we misinterpret because we don't hear about it when it does come to pass. I have given certain prophecies about world events, but because people didn't hear about that event on the news or in some other report, they automatically assumed it wasn't true. If we are going to rightly judge the word, we need to make very certain we hear it carefully, make sure we fully understand the message, and then pray about it.

I have also seen people misinterpret prophecy because of the timing. Because the word didn't happen in the time frame they thought it would, they assumed the word was erroneous.

WORDS THAT DON'T FALL TO THE GROUND

On one occasion, when I was being interviewed about the prophetic, the interviewer made this statement: "I want prophets who are like Samuel, whose words never fell to the ground. Where are the Samuel prophets today whose words don't fall to the ground?" He was referring to the verse written about the prophetic words of Samuel the prophet: "So Samuel grew, and the LORD was with him and let none of his words fall to the ground" (1 Samuel 3:19). The interviewer made this comment because he truly wanted to receive from prophets who were accurate, and there is nothing wrong with that. I, along with everyone else, want that too. But many have understood this verse to imply that prophets should never make mistakes in their prophesying. However, this understanding has placed unjust and wrongful expectations on prophets and those who desire to minister the secrets of God.

I responded to the interviewer's statement along these lines: "If this was the doctrinal requirement or standard for prophets and the prophetic, then my question is, does that mean Elisha, Elijah, Moses, Aaron, Abraham, Jonah, Ezekiel, Daniel, Joel, Amos, Obadiah, Jeremiah, Isaiah, Nathan, John the Baptist, and the apostle Paul, just to name a few prophets, were all false? You see, the Bible never records that these prophets' words never fell to the ground! Does this make them false or even wrong prophets because that was never said about them?"

I too once believed this idea about prophets, but when I looked deeper into this idea, I realized that Samuel was the only prophet in the Bible about whom this was said. If that was a biblical requirement for all prophets, then this should have been said about many of the other celebrated prophets in Scripture.

Many have used that verse to say you can never miss it because Samuel didn't. Well, did he ever miss it? Was he ever wrong and subject to making a mistake? Think back again to 1 Samuel 16 when he was sent to Jesse's sons to anoint the next king of Israel. Do you remember that he started to anoint Eliab until the Lord stopped him? Although he got it right in the end by anointing David, initially he was on the wrong path prophetically, and it took a divine interruption to redirect him.

I believe this statement about Samuel's words not falling to the ground was used to describe the accuracy and rarity of his prophetic gift. Keep in mind that Samuel was a unique prophet for his day. Let's see what the Bible says about him. "Then the boy Samuel ministered to the LORD before Eli. And the word of the LORD was rare in those days; there was no widespread revelation" (1 Samuel 3:1). We find here that the word of the Lord was scarce and there was no open revelation because of the corruption and compromise of Eli the priest and his sons, which we read about in 1 Samuel 2:22–23: "Now Eli was very old; and he heard everything his sons did to all Israel, and how they lay with the women who assembled at the door of the tabernacle of meeting. So he said to them, 'Why do you do such things? For I hear of your evil dealings from all the people.'"

The sinful environment in Israel had nearly shut down the operation of the prophetic ministry, which made Samuel a unique gift. For the first time in a long time, someone was beginning to prophesy again with purity. Without question, God not only anointed Samuel for this time in history, but God also placed a special protection over Samuel, who would have to forge some new ground to bring about this fresh prophetic season. God was making sure that every word this young prophet spoke was carefully watched over and protected. The King James Version of 1 Samuel 3:1 says, "The word of the LORD was precious in those days." It had to be cared for like a precious piece of crystal. I believe God took special care of Samuel's prophecies because Samuel was just about the only one available anywhere to speak for God at that time.

I think of it like starting a campfire when you go camping. At the beginning stage, you have to give the kindling extra care. You create a small spark, then some smoke rises, and you might even blow on the fire and give extra effort to support it until it gets strong. Then, as the blaze builds, it continues getting stronger until it no longer needs the same intensive care. I think this was the exact picture in Samuel's day, and God was giving extra care to the fledgling fire of the prophetic to restore its correct operation in the land.

Young Samuel was still growing (1 Samuel 3:19) and was still fragile as a prophet—just as the restoration of the prophetic was still fragile.

Not only was he still young in age, but he also didn't have a lot of people from whom to draw support. God was still developing him into a trusted, accurate prophet who could handle what God had called him to do.

Our goal should be to have a high standard for accuracy in the prophetic. I believe that just as Samuel helped to restore the prophetic flow in his day, we need to strive for his level of accuracy. We need the proper environment and constant training for that to happen. But I am also convinced that Samuel's example is not meant to imply that one can't make honest mistakes. Putting such a restriction—or any other unnecessary restrictions, judgments, and standards—on ourselves or on the prophetic can make us fearful to prophesy anything.

STONE THAT PROPHET

If we cannot determine a true or false prophet based only on the accuracy of his or her prophecy, then how do we know a false prophet from a true one? There are some scriptures that show us how, but people have often ignored them and held to the idea that *one wrong prophecy means a false prophet*. Once they determine you are false, look out for a modern-day stoning! Today it isn't with actual stones but, rather, a verbal assault of criticism. I want to review these Scripture verses about false prophets closely so we can understand what they say.

Let's begin by defining the word *false*. There is a vast difference between *false* and *wrong*. Something that is *false* carries the connotation of "counterfeit" and "trickery." It intends to deceive. Someone who is *wrong* may not intend to deceive whatsoever; that person just made a human error. So when we refer to false prophets, we need to identify a person whose primary intent *and* regular activity is to lead people astray, whether doctrinally, financially, or for some other purpose.

There are several scriptures that refer to false prophets. As we look at these, we will discover that the accuracy of the prophecy had little to do with whether or not it was delivered by true or false prophets. In fact, there were as many false prophets who produced miracles and prophesied accurately as there were true prophets. Even Pharaoh's magicians could do supernatural things.

Other prophets started out right, but their motives and heart intents became tainted, and they entered the ranks of the false later on. The Bible referred to Balaam as one of those. He started as a true prophet and then went the way of error by using his prophetic anointing for an evil and harmful purpose. Notice what the Bible says about him: "They have forsaken the right way and gone astray, following the way of Balaam the son of Beor, who loved the wages of unrighteousness" (2 Peter 2:15). The Book of Revelation expands by saying:

> But I have a few things against you, because you have there those who hold the doctrine of Balaam, who taught Balak to put a stumbling block before the children of Israel, to eat things sacrificed to idols, and to commit sexual immorality.
>
> —REVELATION 2:14

In spite of the fact that Balaam was in terrible error, many of his prophecies were true. He prophesied many things correctly concerning Israel, more so than some of the other prophets. He was a true prophet who became a false prophet because he developed a deceptive and evil intent—although his prophecies were accurate. He chose to compromise his gift, contrary to what God wanted for him.

Before we cast our verbal *false prophet stones*, we better make sure we know what it is that we are hurling our rocks at! Jesus taught that only the sinless had the right to cast stones (John 8:7), but many people still feel that prophets who make mistakes should be classified as false and should be subject to strict and sometimes harsh church disciplinary measures. Deuteronomy 13 helps us to understand why some people develop a misguided view about true and false prophets. It also gives us direction for how we should correctly respond to both:

If there arises among you a prophet or a dreamer of dreams, and he gives you a sign or a wonder, and the sign or the wonder comes to pass, of which he spoke to you, saying, "Let us go after other gods"—which you have not known—"and let us serve them," you shall not listen to the words of that prophet or that dreamer of dreams, for the LORD your God is testing you to know whether you love the LORD your God with all your heart and with all your soul. You shall walk after the LORD your God and fear Him, and keep His commandments and obey His voice, and you shall serve Him and hold fast to Him. But that prophet or that dreamer of dreams shall be put to death, because he has spoken in order to turn you away from the LORD your God, who brought you out of the land of Egypt and redeemed you from the house of bondage, to entice you from the way in which the LORD your God commanded you to walk. So you shall put away the evil from your midst.

—DEUTERONOMY 13:1–5

Notice that the prophet had dreams and miracles that actually *did* come to pass. In other words, they were accurate prophetic revelations. Yet the fruit of his life and message was to draw people away from the Lord into serving other gods. He drew their love and attention away from God. This is what made him and others like him false prophets. The determining factor of one being a true or false prophet was not at all based on a failed or successful prophecy, but rather on his false behavior, which attempted to turn people away from God. The prophet who was false actually used true signs, revelation, and wonders to draw people into worshiping other things besides the Lord. This is very different from a true prophet of God who may have missed it or made a mistake.

This type of false prophet was to be put to death, often by stoning (verse 5). Why did they stone him? Because he drew people away from

God and wanted to deceive them. Stoning wasn't for the true prophet who may have missed it, misspoke, or made an honest mistake. True prophets need to be trained and developed, while it is false prophets who need to be disciplined and removed from their places of influence.

In the Old Testament, false prophets were put to death, often by stoning. Stoning was not just limited to false prophets but also included those who committed adultery and other sinful acts: "The man who commits adultery with another's wife, even his neighbor's wife, the adulterer and the adulteress shall surely be put to death" (Leviticus 20:10, AMP). Deuteronomy 22 tells us how they were to die:

> If a man is found lying with a woman married to a husband, then both of them shall die—the man that lay with the woman, and the woman; so you shall put away the evil from Israel. If a young woman who is a virgin is betrothed to a husband, and a man finds her in the city and lies with her, then you shall bring them both out to the gate of that city, and you shall stone them to death with stones, the young woman because she did not cry out in the city, and the man because he humbled his neighbor's wife; so you shall put away the evil from among you.
>
> —DEUTERONOMY 22:22-24

In reality, under this same law, King David should have been stoned for his adultery with Bathsheba. This same law should have applied to Aaron the priest, who did what a false prophet does: he used his words, money, and worldly possessions to draw people away from God to worship a golden calf. The Law of God was fresh in the hands of Moses as he came down from the mountain. According to the Law Moses received, his brother Aaron was now guilty of being a false prophet and punishable by death! The Lord had declared that Aaron was a prophet (Exodus 7:1). There was no better time to enforce this Law, was there?

The penalty of stoning or being put to death was not limited just to prophets. Look at this next set of verses:

> If your brother, the son of your mother, your son or your daughter, the wife of your bosom, or your friend who is as your own soul, secretly entices you, saying, "Let us go and serve other gods," which you have not known, neither you nor your fathers, of the gods of the people which are all around you, near to you or far off from you, from one end of the earth to the other end of the earth, you shall not consent to him or listen to him, nor shall your eye pity him, nor shall you spare him or conceal him; but you shall surely kill him; your hand shall be first against him to put him to death, and afterward the hand of all the people. And you shall stone him with stones until he dies, because he sought to entice you away from the LORD your God, who brought you out of the land of Egypt, from the house of bondage. So all Israel shall hear and fear, and not again do such wickedness as this among you.
> —DEUTERONOMY 13:6–11

The death sentence for a false prophet also applied to any relative who drew people away from God. It is interesting that when people want to call for the modern-day stoning of a "false prophet," they never mention any of their relatives who have tried to draw them away from church, criticized their Christianity, or even drawn them into sinful activities. Typically, we are slower to apply the same methods of church discipline when things get closer to home. Not even Aaron, Moses's brother, who actually did the things that made him guilty of being a false prophet, was stoned according to the Law.

As we can see, if we *stone* or discipline false prophets, then we have to apply the same rules to others who fall into the mentioned sins. To suggest that this requirement was only for prophets would be wrong. We also need to be very careful when applying this disciplinary approach to be sure it is actually a false prophet to whom we are applying it. It is not a disciplinary standard for those who truly minister as an honest prophet in the secrets of God and yet occasionally give a wrong prophecy.

FALSE PROPHET OR FALSE IDENTIFICATION?

In 1 Kings 22, the Bible talks about the four hundred prophets who all told King Ahab the same thing: God wanted him to fight against Ramoth Gilead. However, there was one more prophet named Micaiah who prophesied the opposite of the other four hundred. He said that the Lord *did not* want King Ahab to fight against Ramoth Gilead. If he did, the result would be that Israel would be scattered on the mountains and the king would be killed.

Micaiah's words proved to be true. The other prophets had given a false or wrong prophecy, which could have had catastrophic results. The Bible never records that the four hundred prophets were stoned or even disciplined for their wrong prophecies.

The false prophets spoken of in Ezekiel 13 and Jeremiah 23 were not put to death either for their lying words and visions. According to the Law, if their intent had been to draw people away from the Lord, they probably should have been stoned. Instead, they were corrected and reprimanded by another method.

What am I saying, then? We can't be quick to jump to criticism or even discipline of those who prophesy, because sometimes it may take time to know if the prophecy was truly from God or it was simply spoken in error. In fact, the prophecies from many of the prophets of the Old Testament didn't even come to pass in their lifetimes. I am sure this looked false or wrong to some. Others were even accused of such. It is amazing that in the Old Testament, it seems the people let the prophets who really did sinful things slip without discipline, but they wanted to run the ones who were righteous out of town and kill them!

Deuteronomy 18 refers to false prophets and prophecy. These verses help us to see what to do if a true minister for Jesus Christ delivers a wrong word.

> But a prophet who presumes to speak in my name anything I have not commanded him to say, or a prophet who speaks in the name of other gods, must be put to death. You may say to yourselves, "How can we know when a message has not been spoken by the LORD?" If what a prophet proclaims in the name of the LORD does not take place or come true, that is a message the LORD has not spoken. That prophet has spoken presumptuously. Do not be afraid of him.
> —DEUTERONOMY 18:20–22, NIV

People sometimes say, "See here? If the prophet speaks in God's name falsely, he was to receive discipline!" However, let me draw your focus to verse 20, which states, "A prophet *who presumes to speak in my name…*" (emphasis added). In the Hebrew, it literally means to boil up in arrogance and rebellion. That doesn't sound like an honest and true prophet, does it? This verse applies to those prophets who are defiant against God and commit to false gods or doctrines.

Verse 22 gives reassurance that should abate any fear of receiving or hearing a simple wrong prophecy from a true prophet. In a nutshell, the verse says that if someone comes along who upholds the Lord's name, we should not be fearful of him if he makes a mistake. It is an honest mistake, and if his prophecy doesn't come to pass, or he speaks out of turn, don't sweat it! Your safety lies in the fact that his heart is for the Lord and his intention is to do the right thing.

Too often we are quick to jump to conclusions about whether or not a true prophet's words actually came to pass. Perhaps the word *did* come to pass, and we just didn't know it. Or perhaps the person receiving the word did something to hinder it from happening. For example, if someone receives a prophecy about a new job that is on its way but that person never gets one because he or she stays home all day being lazy and waiting for it to manifest, then the blame does not fall to God's ministers for the outcome.

Many prophecies in Scripture didn't appear to come to pass in the lifetimes of the people who heard them. Instead, they came to pass after their lifetime. Other examples are given of prophecies that were spoken as absolutes, but circumstance and human choice changed the outcome. Let's look at a few of these examples:

- Isaiah prophesied that King Hezekiah would die (Isaiah 38:1–5). Notice there were no conditions attached when the word was given. I am sure the average onlooker could have thought that prophecy was false when Hezekiah lived another fifteen years. I am further certain that some may have thought, "Oh, the prophet is changing his prophecy now, because Hezekiah didn't die."

- Jonah prophesied that Nineveh would be judged and destroyed in forty days (Jonah 3:4). You and I both know that if such a word was given today, and it didn't happen just like it was said, people would scream, "False prophet!" When Jonah gave this word, no additional conditions for repentance were given. The prophet simply said the city was going to be overthrown, and that's it. I am sure there were those who thought Jonah was a false prophet when it didn't happen, all because they didn't get the new report that Nineveh had repented, so God changed His mind and didn't destroy the city as prophesied.

This is why we have to be careful. If we are going to be quick to stone or discipline prophets, then we also need the same standard for other ministry gifts in the body of Christ. I am sure every pastor has preached things out of a lack of biblical understanding, and later they wished they hadn't preached it! Each of us is growing in God, and we need to give people in the prophetic the same opportunity for growth without the fear of accusation and criticism.

Have you ever prayed for someone to be healed and they didn't get healed? Does that make you a false healer? Of course not; you are just growing and learning to be used by God. If you witness to someone and they don't get saved, that doesn't make you a false evangelist, does it? Or, if you make an honest mistake in your ability to interpret Scripture and teach something incorrect to others, does that make you a false teacher? The New Testament actually speaks more about false teachers than it does about false prophets.

How, then, do we recognize a false prophet today? Jesus mentioned that we would know them by their fruits. Second Peter gives us a list of the fruits or characteristics of a false prophet.

> But there were also false prophets among the people, even as there will be false teachers among you, who will secretly bring in destructive heresies, even denying the Lord who bought them, and bring on themselves swift destruction.
>
> —2 Peter 2:1

Take a look at the false fruit mentioned in the second chapter of 2 Peter:

- False prophets bring in damnable heresies, messages, and teachings (verse 1).

- They deny the Lord (verse 1).

- They are covetous, and their words make merchandise of people (verse 3).

- They walk in the flesh (verse 10).

- False prophets despise authority (verse 10).

- They are presumptuous and not Holy Spirit led (verse 10).

- They speak evil of dignitaries (verse 10).

- They are immoral, and their eyes are full of adultery (verse 14).

- They can't cease from sin (verse 14).

- They go after unstable or young Christians and people (verse 14).

- They go the way of Balaam, using witchcraft and compromise (verse 15).

- They speak swelling, convincing words meant to deceive (verse 18).

These verses identify the fruit of false prophets. We need to be doctrinally correct and able to discern those who teach the Word of God and minister prophetically from those who exhibit false fruit. We must be able to measure the message of every prophet against the Bible.

MATURING IN THE PROPHETIC

It has not been my intention to excuse false prophets. No one should make a habit of prophesying words that don't come to pass and continue to pass it off as just making mistakes. We should all strive for the highest level of accuracy in receiving and delivering the secrets of God. If we are receiving those prophecies, we need to keep a receptive attitude toward God's true prophetic ministers. If we don't understand a prophecy at the time it is delivered, then we need to hold on to it and see if God reveals its meaning to us over time.

Before we started our church, a proven prophetic minister once prophesied over my wife and me. He prophesied that we were called to pastor, and, I tell you, we both thought this minister missed God! At the time, we felt no desire to pastor a church. But we kept it in the back of our minds. It was seven years later when we started our church. Seven years! This person didn't miss it, and the prophecy was true; we just needed to align ourselves with the will of God.

Under the Mosaic Law, people were stoned as a form of punishment. But when Jesus was confronted with the angry crowd who wanted to stone the woman caught in adultery, He taught, "He who is without sin among you, let him throw a stone at her first" (John 8:7). The Greek definition for *sin* is to miss the mark. Jesus was saying to the religious Pharisees that according to the Mosaic Law, they could throw stones at this woman caught in adultery, but they could only throw such stones if they themselves never sinned or missed it.

Jesus was implying that a new dispensation of grace would be the standard for the New Testament church. It was not a license to continue in wrongdoing (Romans 6:1). Instead, grace speaks of love, forgiveness, and the chance to minister for the Lord as a vessel of honor, even though you have human frailties. Jesus was also implying that we all miss it from time to time, and there is grace to try again and sin no more.

Don't purposely use your gift to sin as the false prophet does, but if you make a mistake, don't condemn yourself; God's grace will cover you.

The apostle Paul even mentioned that he became a minister because of God's grace to him (Ephesians 3:7). He had shortcomings and made mistakes. But his motive, purpose, and daily quest were to do right in serving God. There is grace for you to step out and try in the prophetic. The key is to stay pure and submitted to others. As you learn to walk in God's anointing, you will stand with those who reveal the true secrets of the Lord.

SEVEN

PROPHETS: GOD'S PREPARED GIFT TO THE CHURCH

Then I asked the angel, "What about the olive trees on each side of the lampstand? What do they represent? And what is the meaning of the two branches from which golden olive oil flows through the two gold pipes?" "Don't you know?" he asked. "No sir, I don't," was my answer. Then he told me, "These branches are the two chosen leaders who stand beside the Lord of all the earth."

–Zechariah 4:11–14, CEV

W HERE IS THE WIND?" I THOUGHT AS I TOSSED AND TURNED, trying to sleep. The truth was that I couldn't sleep because of a word I had prophesied. Earlier that evening during a church service where I was the guest minister, I told the audience that the Lord was going to give them a sign because He wanted to show them that the prophetic was still much alive today. They were having a little trouble having confidence in modern-day prophets. I had felt the Lord instructing me along these lines earlier in the day when I was praying in my hotel. The word I prophesied to them was that after midnight that evening, the winds would begin blowing very strong in the city and there would be thunder and lightning but no rain. I told them that these winds would be a sign to this church and city that the winds of change were coming and that God still uses the prophetic today.

Well, it was after midnight, and no wind! There wasn't a creature stirring, not even a mouse! There was no wind, lightning, or thunder. You can imagine the rush of thoughts trying to hit my mind. The minutes seemed like hours. I got up and looked out of the window of the hotel, and it was so nice and quiet. Things looked to be the very opposite of what I said. I looked at the clock and then my watch to make sure it was indeed after midnight. Well, it was after midnight, but no wind. So I did what most of us would do—I prayed real hard. Of course, I asked the Lord what was going on.

Finally, I decided to try to settle back to sleep. I must have dozed off, only to be startled by the noise outside. I was thrilled to find that it was extremely windy! "Thanks, Lord!" That illustrates how a prophet can feel when his or her reputation is on the line.

The next day, the pastor of the church talked about the prophetic word from the night before. He mentioned the part about God intending to give them a sign. Well, not only did they get a sign from the winds blowing furiously, but also the sign on their church was blown off their building and landed in the street! Now that gives a new meaning to seeing a *sign*! Afterward, they were much more excited about prophets, to say the least. I was happy because God wants to use prophets today.

THE TWO OLIVE TREES

We know that God doesn't have to prove the validity of the prophetic ministry, but God will promote prophets and their message. Even if some have lost confidence in the prophetic because of some of the careless behavior that has gone on with prophetic things, God still believes in prophets.

Zechariah had a vision that emphasized the importance of the prophetic ministry in every generation. Yes, that's right; the prophetic is *needed*! Let's go to Zechariah 4:11: "Then I answered and said to him, 'What are these two olive trees—at the right of the lampstand and at its left?'" Zechariah was asking about the two olive trees that he saw in the vision. Obviously, the trees were some kind of mystery to him or he wouldn't have had to ask about them. Surely, he knew they were trees, but he didn't know what they meant or why they were there. They had a prophetic meaning, and Zechariah wanted to know what it was.

The angel gave him an initial answer by saying, "These are the two anointed ones, who stand beside the Lord of the whole earth" (verse 14). You might already be thinking that the angel's answer didn't provide a lot of information. However, the mystery of these two trees—the two anointed ones—is unveiled throughout Scripture. As we journey through it, you will not only receive a better revelation of the power that comes through the prophetic, but you will also want to help promote its operation in your own life and wherever else God wants to use it.

The Book of Revelation gives us a great deal of insight:

> These are the two olive trees and the two lampstands standing before the God of the earth. And if anyone wants to harm them, fire proceeds from their mouth and devours their enemies. And if anyone wants to harm them, he must be killed in this manner. These have power to shut heaven, so that no rain falls in the days of their prophecy; and they have power over waters to turn them to blood, and to strike the earth with all plagues, as often as they desire.
>
> —REVELATION 11:4-6

We find the trees to be two very anointed individuals, and they are actually the two famous witnesses in Revelation who stood and prophesied for three and a half years. Imagine three and a half years packed with their prophecies! In other words, God established two powerful prophets in order to bring a strong presence of prophetic input into the events of the day.

Notice that these two had the power to control weather elements. They were able to speak to the heavens that there would be no rain and to strike the earth's waters, turning them to blood. You can probably already see that the things they did here mimic the ministries of both Moses and Elijah. Elijah prophesied there would be no rain (1 Kings 17:1), and Moses turned water into blood (Exodus 7:15–17).

When we read and interpret the Bible, it is important to remember that we can view it three ways, all of which are important. We can view it historically, seeing the events as they actually happened. We can see a literal meaning, which is illustrated by the way we apply the written Word to our lives. Finally, there is a prophetic meaning, which often reveals a hidden meaning.

For example, the two olive trees were literal olive trees, but they carried a hidden prophetic meaning that was something else. In fact, when we think of an olive, we think of the oil it produces. Prophetically, that oil is representative of the anointing; the trees speak of people who are rooted and grounded. This reveals the olive trees as an anointing that comes upon people.

You can often pull prophetic meaning from much of Scripture if you study it carefully. Because prophetic revelation is the focus of this book, by looking closer we can see why God needs the prophetic to operate regularly today.

Some biblical theologians suggest that Revelation 11:4–6 is only a literal event relating to the End Times. They believe that it refers to the two witnesses who will be revealed in the days of the Great Tribulation. That is most certainly true, but I want us to see these same verses in light of prophetic interpretation.

Because of the similarities in ministry, we can easily see that these two witnesses point to the ministries of Moses and Elijah, even though it may not actually be Moses and Elijah who are raised from the dead in this passage. I want to focus our thinking on the anointing these two witnesses carried. When those who are anointed by God die, the anointing of the Holy Spirit that rested upon them remains in the earth to bless and help the generations who follow them. When an anointed ministry vessel finishes his or her race and goes on to heaven, God will always raise up others who will take the anointing that person had and manifest it through others. They may not present that anointing in the exact way the previous person did, but it is what that particular anointing accomplishes that we need.

Throughout Scripture we can see the unique anointing of Moses and Elijah continually manifested and present. Then, in the Book of Revelation, it comes to its final culmination. If their anointing was evident throughout the Bible, and will be in the End Times, I also believe it is still manifesting in the church today.

We find Moses and Elijah, these two olive trees, together in another example on the Mount of Transfiguration:

> And He [Jesus] was transfigured before them. His face shone like the sun, and His clothes became as white as the light. And behold, Moses and Elijah appeared to them, talking with Him.
>
> —MATTHEW 17:2–3

In Zechariah 4:14, the two olives trees—or better said, the anointing of Moses and Elijah—were standing before the Lord. It is interesting that in Jesus's transfiguration they were once again standing beside the Lord, just as in the vision of Zechariah.

What does an Elijah and Moses type of anointing represent? They paint a picture of the apostolic and prophetic ministries, with Jesus standing in the center as the head of His church. They demonstrate the ministry of the apostle and prophet—foundational ministries of the church.

> Now, therefore, you are no longer strangers and
> foreigners, but fellow citizens with the saints and
> members of the household of God, having been built
> on the foundation of the apostles and prophets, Jesus
> Christ Himself being the chief cornerstone.
> —EPHESIANS 2:19–20

Not only is the church built literally upon the foundation laid by the apostles and prophets in the Bible, but it also continues to be built upon the foundation of the modern-day anointing of these two ministries as well, just as it has been throughout the generations.

Moses, the first olive tree, was the apostle who built the tabernacle of God's presence. The word *apostle* means sent one. Sent to do what? Apostles are sent to build. Those who functioned in the apostle's anointing in Bible times built things that others could benefit from. That could include physical buildings, but it also includes spiritual ones. A spiritual house could be a church, a missions' outreach that governs a region, or a Bible school. It involves more than just being a missionary, as some have suggested. It indicates becoming the actual mission center from which missionaries can come and go. Do you see the difference? It is more than just starting a church and being the pastor; it is building a church that extends beyond the church setting and provides a foundation that develops and empowers other churches and ministries. This is why apostles aren't just sent; they are sent to build. The church would cease to function without these builders operating.

Elijah, the second olive tree, represents the prophetic ministry. The prophet's role is a foundational ministry because it gets plans and blueprints for heaven and puts the heart and presence of God into the building process. In the Book of Ezra, Cyrus, a type of an apostle, decreed that the temple be rebuilt. In Ezra 5:2 we see that when the builders began to build, the prophets of God were there helping them! How were they helping? They were adding God's voice into the process by prophesying. They were constantly telling the builders what was on God's mind for the next phase in building. They were expressing the emotions of God and revealing His plan. They also gave warnings from God.

The prophets added a dimension of God's presence through their vocal, demonstrative, and expressive anointing. You cannot build anything for God without the dimension of God's voice, which comes specifically through the prophetic. While we can all hear from God in our own lives, we still need prophets to speak collectively so the church can be unified in its purpose. For example, when a prophet gives a word to a church as a whole, it helps that church to make a unified effort to accomplish something significant. Prophets can bring clarity to things we may be hearing from God. This is why we can't eliminate or overlook the dimension of prophets in anything we do.

From this we can conclude that Moses and Elijah represent the two foundational ministries of the apostle and prophet, and we cannot function effectively as Christians, or as the church, without either. But the most powerful revelation in this prophetic picture is Jesus Christ standing in the middle; He is what holds the entire structure together. Apostles and prophets should not draw attention to themselves; they should point to Jesus and seek to make Him the center of attention. He is the *chief cornerstone*! These two ministries are a part of the foundation upon which the church can depend, but Jesus is the foundational fulcrum—the original building block upon which everything else is dependent.

THE IMPORTANCE OF FOUNDATIONS

Foundations are critically important foundations—without a foundation, it is impossible to build properly. As I was praying one afternoon, the Lord showed me a pastor I knew who was in a building project for his church. In a vision I saw a set of blueprints with pillars and noticed the foundation under one of the pillars. In the vision, I could see the exact placement of this pillar on the blueprints, and I sensed something was wrong with the section of foundation near that particular pillar.

When I called the pastor of this church and described my vision, he said that he didn't know if anything was wrong but would check to make sure. He said it was important that I had accurately sensed that something was wrong because it would cost some money to look into it. When he had the building site examined, he discovered some real problems in the exact area of the pillar I had seen. It could have been even more costly had they not checked it, because the foundation was compromised. It could have created a number of problems for them in the future.

I am sure you can already see the spiritual principle I am driving at in this example. When the foundation is not properly built, although we may not see any repercussions immediately, eventually, when the earth beneath settles and the building shifts and is subjected to adverse weather, problems will arise. I am convinced that there are many problems in the church today that could have been avoided had we built our ministries on the right apostolic and prophetic foundations.

There are other biblical examples of these two foundational ministries:

- *The two olive trees*—Moses (apostolic) and Elijah (prophetic) (Zechariah 4; Matthew 17; Ephesians 2:20; Revelation 11)

- *Moses and Aaron*—Moses, a type of apostle, was a sent one and builder, and Aaron was to be his prophet (Exodus 7:1).

- *The axe head and the handle*—The axe is used for building (apostolic), and the handle helps in the process of building (prophetic) (2 Kings 6).

- *The two trumpets*—One trumpet was used for gathering (apostolic) and the other for warning (prophetic) (Numbers 10).

- *The hammer and the sword*—The hammer is a building tool (apostolic), and the sword was for warring (prophetic) (Nehemiah 4:17–18).

- *The pillars of cloud and fire*—The cloud (apostolic) covers, protects, and moves the church. The fire (prophetic) reveals those things hidden in darkness. Moses (apostolic) fellowshiped with God in a cloud, and Elijah (prophetic) met God in a chariot of fire (Exodus 13:21–22; 2 Kings 2:11).

Other examples of the two olive tree ministries of the apostle and prophet can be found in the literal sense of Scripture as well. Paul (an apostle) and Barnabas (a prophet) traveled as a team (Acts 13:1). The name *Barnabas* is Chaldean and means "son of Nabas," or literally, the son of prophecy. Additionally, Acts 4:36 tells us his surname, Joses, was interpreted as "the son of consolation." Some translations say *encouragement*. One of the primary purposes of prophecy is to encourage (1 Corinthians 14:3). So there is little doubt that Paul and Barnabas functioned as an apostolic and prophetic team.

The apostle Paul also traveled with Silas, whom Scripture said was a prophet (Acts 15:32).

These apostolic and prophetic ministry teams claimed new territory for the Lord and imparted God's anointing as they preached the kingdom of God. Tremendous power is released when these two ministries—the two olive trees—are functioning together. Undoubtedly, one of the reasons Paul had such an effective ministry was because he had a prophet working alongside him.

I am not implying that every ministry or apostle must have a personal prophet as a sidekick. Sure, when prophets and apostles work closely together, it is a powerful thing, but that doesn't mean God requires you to have an apostle and prophet duo. What I am saying, however, is that every ministry needs a degree of prophetic input, expression, and involvement. Then, in turn, every ministry also needs an apostolic source and connection from which to feed and to be in relationship with. These things will help keep the foundation of the ministry strong and on course as it is being built. Be sure the foundation of the two ministries and their anointing are present in your ministry and your life.

The devil hates these foundational ministries and has sought to minimize and even exclude them. He knows the power of a good foundation too. A good example of the enemy's desire to destroy this prototype is found in 2 Kings, where a wicked king named Ahaz compromised the setup of Solomon's temple.

> And King Ahaz cut off the panels of the carts, and removed the lavers from them; and he took down the Sea from the bronze oxen that were under it, and put it on a pavement of stones.
>
> —2 KINGS 16:17

When Solomon's house was built, it was equipped with a molten sea (2 Chronicles 4:2–6), which actually was a large water basin made of molten metal fifteen feet across and seven and a half feet deep. It was almost the size of a swimming pool. This giant sea bath was the place of cleansing, particularly for the priests, and it sat on a stone foundation of twelve oxen. In this example, the molten sea speaks of a place of cleansing, which is the church. In Scripture we often find that oxen point to the apostolic ministry, which we won't try to explain in detail here. Twelve is also the number of the kingdom. Jesus placed His church on an apostolic foundation of kingdom order.

However, King Ahaz moved this molten sea from this foundation of oxen and set it upon a different foundation of pavement. Prophetically, that tells us the devil wants nothing more than to remove the church from its apostolic foundation. This is exactly what religion and tradition have done with the apostolic and prophetic foundations of the church. They have cut off these two vital ministries by saying they no longer exist and have passed away. They also remove them by giving them no place or voice in churches or ministries today.

Yet, Jesus told us that if we would receive a true prophet of the Lord, we would receive a prophet's reward (Matthew 10:41). In other words, we receive a blessing from the prophet's ministry. One of those rewards is receiving the secrets of the Lord.

Jesus emphasizes the importance of receiving the two olive tree ministries of the apostolic and prophetic in the Gospels by sending out His prophets and apostles. However, even then, the people did not receive them.

> Therefore the wisdom of God also said, "I will send them prophets and apostles, and some of them they will kill and persecute," that the blood of all the prophets which was shed from the foundation of the world may be required of this generation, from the blood of Abel to the blood of Zechariah who perished between the altar and the temple. Yes, I say to you, it shall be required of this generation.
>
> —LUKE 11:49–51

It is a very serious matter to reject or persecute a true apostle or prophet of the Lord. God did not think highly of those who rejected prophets. The generation mentioned above rejected and persecuted God's true prophets. Jesus told them that the blood of Abel all the way to Zechariah was required of them!

How is it different for us today? We may not be literally killing God's prophets, but in some circles we are certainly killing the operation of prophets and this anointing. I don't think in God's mind it is much different, because we are limiting an important foundational anointing that He designed for the church.

You may be thinking, "Yes, but the prophets of the Bible were not like the prophets today with all their issues and wrong behavior!" I think we have established the fact that even the prophets of the Bible had human frailties. However, human frailty today cannot be an excuse to throw out the prophetic expression altogether. God still has confidence in prophets, even though they are not perfect vessels. We need prophets today, and we must not be like others in this generation who persecute or reject prophets or the anointing of the prophetic.

Prophets Are Servants

As one of the olive-tree, foundational ministries, the prophetic calling is a gift from the Lord to serve the needs of others. God so deeply believes in the ministry of His prophets that He wants to discuss all His plans with them before He carries them out in the earth.

> Surely the Lord GOD does nothing, unless He reveals
> His secret to His servants the prophets.
> —Amos 3:7

This verse says God will do nothing unless He talks first to a prophet. It also identifies God's prophets as "His servants." God wants us to see the prophetic ministry not as a ministry of arrogance and prominence but, rather, as a ministry that serves the kingdom in humility. Prophets do this by encouraging, comforting, and strengthening people with the secrets of the Lord, which they exhibit through a servant's heart.

Jesus was the first great example of a servant. The Bible says that He humbled Himself and took on the form of a servant (Philippians 2:7). He set the precedent for the rest of us. The more we use our gift to serve others in love, humility, and unselfishness, the more we will receive His secrets.

Prophets vs. Prophetic People

Not everyone is called to be a prophet. Prophets are those whom God has chosen to stand in an office of ministry. We are, however, called to be a prophetic people who support and cultivate a prophetic environment. We can do that primarily by involving the ministry of the prophet. We can also do that by raising up believers who can be used to prophesy. We can even increase the atmosphere of the prophetic through music (1 Chronicles 25:1). In 1 Samuel 10:5, we find a company of prophets who came with instruments of music and began to prophesy while playing them. As a result, even Saul began to prophesy in that atmosphere (verse 11). The right music can pull the prophetic out of the people.

The prophet's office and call come with a higher level of responsibility because a higher level of God's secrets will be revealed to them on a regular basis. Certainly God can use everyday believers to receive high-level secrets, and He does do that. But with the prophet, God gives these kinds of plans and secrets on a regular basis because it is part of their job description.

Just because someone prophesies does not mean that person is a prophet. Some are prophets while others will simply be used to prophesy. Notice the verse below:

> And He Himself gave...some prophets.
> —EPHESIANS 4:11

Since God did give some prophets, then we need to make room for them. Who are we to say we don't need them when God gave them? "And God has appointed these in the church: first apostles, second prophets, third teachers, after that miracles, then gifts of healings, helps, administrations, varieties of tongues" (1 Corinthians 12:28). God *set them* in the church, and we should not remove them. Instead, we should allow their ministry to have a place. Churches that eliminate the ministry of the prophets—or any of the things God set in the church, for that matter—will eventually become void of God's power and find themselves resembling more of a social gathering that lacks the demonstration of the Holy Spirit.

Through my years of ministry, I have come to realize how much the prophetic office is misunderstood. I have also learned the heavy responsibility and testing that come with being called to the prophet's office. I remember the times when God confirmed the prophetic call on my life. At the time, I had no idea the road God would take me on to develop me in the prophet's ministry. That calling did not come by my own self-appointment. It came as the Lord first spoke it into my heart and taught me about prophets in Scripture. Later, it was confirmed through valid, proven ministers and, most importantly, my own pastor. The process for stepping into the calling of a prophet is not always an easy process.

My prophetic calling was confirmed publicly when a minister called me out of an audience as I was just starting in the ministry and spoke to me about the prophetic call on my life. For a while, it seemed that other solid, proven ministers were calling me out to tell me I had a prophetic call to be a prophet at every meeting I attended. I knew God was supernaturally speaking to me and confirming the words of my pastor.

Do you know that even Jesus had prophetic confirmation concerning His calling when the prophet John the Baptist saw Him walking toward the Jordan River to be baptized? John said, "Behold! The Lamb of God who takes away the sin of the world!" (John 1:29). His call was acknowledged and confirmed before witnesses.

I had never asked or wanted to be called to the prophet's ministry. It came during a time when I received persecution from a minister who discouraged me by telling me I was too young and couldn't be called as a prophet. I was only in my early twenties at the time. I never understood this point of view since Jeremiah was called to be a prophet in his mother's womb.

For a season, those words deeply affected me. I felt like I couldn't hear from God or speak for Him. It nearly destroyed my ability to flow in the prophetic things of God. I experienced a lot of persecution, confusion, and heartache during that season of my life. However, during that time I learned a lot about prophets. I learned many lessons in humility and what it means to die to self. You see, sometimes God has to see how low you are willing to bow so He knows how high He can raise you in that call. God was indeed faithful to send those who prophesied to me so that I would not give up on that calling.

This is where many who are called to be prophets miss it. They let others discourage them, so they run like mavericks without being submitted to anyone. They raise themselves up, often with reckless prophetic methods, or they go into seclusion with their gift and give up altogether on God using them. Every true prophet will have to suffer some type of persecution, rejection, feelings of isolation, and misunderstanding. This is all part of the process of maturing into becoming the Lord's spokesman.

THE TRUE PROPHET

Scripture gives us a clear definition of a true prophet. The word *prophet* in the Old Testament Hebrew is *nabiy*, which is simply a man inspired of God. A female is referred to as *prophetess*, which is *nebiyah*, or a woman inspired of God. Any Christian can receive divine inspiration, but a prophet is unique because his inspiration is designed specifically for speaking out and communicating a special message from God.

The Brown-Driver-Briggs Hebrew and English Lexicon states that a prophet's express purpose is to be a *spokesman* or *spokeswoman*. How is he a spokesman? He prophesies the things that God wants to say—and this job becomes a regular requirement for him. *Thayer's Greek Definitions* describes the New Testament prophet as "one who solemnly declares what he has received by inspiration, especially concerning future events." These definitions describe the qualities of a prophet. Other terms used to describe the prophet include "to see, hear, sense, to know by the influence of the Holy Spirit, to empower, instruct, comfort, encourage, convict, discern and foretell certain future events."

I have known some people who suggest a person is identified as a prophet because of a strong personality and temperament. I once knew a man whom many called a prophet because he was a grouch and suppos-edly had a *prophetic temperament*. He viewed things very black and white, very decisively, and exhibited stern behaviors, causing many to draw their conclusions. But according to biblical functions and require-ments, he didn't function in the prophetic office.

Your personality has little to do with your type of calling. Your person-ality only makes your calling special and unique. Prophets, according to the Bible, are those who are called of God to stand in a spiritual office and be God's divinely inspired spokespeople. To say it even more simply: *the man or woman called specifically to be a messenger from God speaks under the divine inspiration of God.*

God communicates to and through prophets with supernatural means, such as visions, dreams, or other biblical spiritual experiences. According to 1 Corinthians 14:3, prophets may also prophesy with the simple gift of prophecy, which is general in nature and uplifts and encourages. But it will often be at a higher level of revelation, authority, insight, and utterance. Prophets, because they are appointed into a ministry office, at times may also speak correction, direction, revelation, instruction, warn-ings, rebukes, and foreknowledge of future events. This is much different than all believers who may prophesy but are not given the positional authority to govern in the church through their prophetic words.

A prophet of the Lord God doesn't select or choose himself or herself. A prophet must be ordained by God and should be confirmed as such by the leadership of a local church or governing body. I have met many who call themselves *prophets* and are not. First, they don't exemplify the necessary anointing or calling to be one. Second, many call them-selves prophets without having been appointed by anyone, and they are not under any type of spiritual authority that judges their words, fruit, character, or lifestyle. They aren't connected to any legitimate church or ministry covering. They may have the call to be a prophet, but they have never been ordained into that position under proper leadership, and often they are very bad examples of true prophets.

Others may be part of a legitimate ministry but try to operate prophetically without their leaders' awareness. I call this type of activity *prophetic covert operations*, or PCOs. One person I knew called himself a prophet and went around feeling the need to visit churches he did not attend. He refused to let anyone speak into his life because he felt no one heard God like he did. So he refused to be part of any ministry. He was not connected to any local church but was in the "traveling" ministry! He felt his calling was to attend a meeting in a different church each week and bring the word of the Lord to that church—often filled with harshness and rebuke. You don't find this in the New Testament churches. It is out of order! The ordained biblical prophets went to the churches to bring words of encouragement and to confirm many things to those they were in relationship with.

Even so, we must remember there are more good prophets of the Lord than bad ones who refuse to be accountable. We have all seen abuses of manipulation and control, and I am not implying or suggesting an over-emphasis on accountability and submission. But we can't reject proper biblical accountability and authority—or prophets—in our churches. The Bible gives clear teaching that prophets are to be ordained and sent under proper, godly authority.

> Now in the church that was at Antioch there were certain prophets and teachers: Barnabas, Simeon who was called Niger, Lucius of Cyrene, Manaen who had been brought up with Herod the tetrarch, and Saul. As they ministered to the Lord and fasted, the Holy Spirit said, "Now separate to Me Barnabas and Saul for the work to which I have called them." Then, having fasted and prayed, and laid hands on them, they sent them away.
>
> –ACTS 13:1–3

Paul, referred to in this verse as Saul, didn't send off for his ordination paper via some ordination company; he was ordained by those who knew him. He didn't title himself and begin handing out his business cards all over Antioch. No, he served as a prophet and a teacher *in the church of Antioch*. He submitted his gift there. Then, when it was good unto the Holy Ghost and the leadership of that church, he was released. In addition, his calling was confirmed and evident to the wider body of Christ.

No two prophets are the same, just as no two people are the same. The Bible tells us that there will be different administrations, operations, and gifts that come with ministering in the Spirit. Just the same, there are different types of prophets.

- Prophets to nations (Jeremiah 1:10)

- Singing prophets and psalmists (1 Samuel 16:23)

- Prophets of events and elements (Acts 11:27; 1 Kings 17:1)

- Prophets to the local church (Acts 13:1)

- Prophets to the body of Christ (Acts 15:32)

- Prophets to individuals (Acts 21:11)

MOUTH-TO-MOUTH

When God speaks through His prophets, He will speak with a method that I like to call *mouth-to-mouth*. This is how God spoke to His servant Moses, and He also spoke to His prophets by this same method.

> Then He said, "Hear now My words:
> If there is a prophet among you,
> I, the LORD, make Myself known to him in a vision;
> I speak to him in a dream.
> Not so with My servant Moses;
> He is faithful in all My house.

I speak with him face to face,
Even plainly, and not in dark sayings;
And he sees the form of the LORD.
Why then were you not afraid
To speak against My servant Moses?"

So the anger of the LORD was aroused against them,
and He departed.

—NUMBERS 12:6–9

When we think of mouth-to-mouth, we think of resuscitation and how it can save the life of a dying person. When one administers mouth-to-mouth, he or she puts their breath into another. Mouth-to-mouth is also a picture of the prophetic. When God speaks mouth to mouth to a prophet, then the prophet can in turn use what God puts in his or her mouth to breathe life into others. We see this in 2 Kings 4 when the son of the Shunammite woman dies. It was the prophet Elisha who restored her child back to life, and he used mouth-to-mouth to make it happen. However, it wasn't just natural mouth-to-mouth but spiritual mouth-to-mouth. It was the breath of the prophetic anointing.

And he went up and lay on the child, and put his mouth on his mouth, his eyes on his eyes, and his hands on his hands; and he stretched himself out on the child, and the flesh of the child became warm. He returned and walked back and forth in the house, and again went up and stretched himself out on him; then the child sneezed seven times, and the child opened his eyes.

—2 KINGS 4:34–35

This child was brought back to life by the prophet's ministry. The mouth of the prophet represents the breath and life of God. Elisha's prophetic act shows us the different expressions used in the prophet's ministry. Mouth-to-mouth speaks of the prophetic ministry as a speaking ministry, giving out the divine breath of God. It is God's words given to the prophet for others through prophecy.

Then we see that Elisha's eyes were put upon the eyes of this child, which speaks of the prophetic as a seeing ministry. This may be in visions and dreams.

The hands of Elisha were upon the hands of the child, representing the ministry of serving. Remember, God's secrets belong to His servants, the prophets.

Last, the stretching forth of himself upon the child implies that the prophetic ministry is meant for the whole body. When ministered in the right spirit, it will revitalize and reheat the body of Christ, as it did with this child. This example reveals that when prophets and prophecy flow correctly, it will give life to individuals, cities, governments, nations, and churches.

Mouth-to-mouth is exactly what the Lord did with Adam as He breathed the breath of life into him. Adam then came to life and became the first spokesman for God. God's speaking mouth to mouth is His breath, voice, and words, which He puts into us to give to others for life and revitalization. And God's mouth-to-mouth impartations reside in His prophets.

The Call to the Secret Place

Mouth-to-mouth is an intimate form of communication. To receive it, we have to set a time and a place to seek the Lord intimately. There is a call to a place of fellowship that every prophetic servant must develop. This is how Moses received the mouth-to-mouth secrets of God. Prophets who are servants of the Lord hear and reveal the secrets of the Lord. One of the vital ways that they receive the word of the Lord is by abiding or staying in the presence of God. This is what I call *the secret place* of His secrets. When the Lord prepares the prophet, He calls him to that secret place to teach him how to receive God's secrets.

I still remember the day when the Lord's voice came to me. I was driving in my car and had been in the ministry for just a few short years. Suddenly, the voice of the Lord spoke something to me that made me pull the car over. It hit me so hard that I began to cry at what I heard the Holy Spirit say. He said, "Hank, I want you to step out of the pulpit for a year. For the next seven years, you will be like Joseph in the Bible and experience many challenges."

My response was, "Why step out of the pulpit for a year, God? Don't You know I am trying to be a traveling minister and that this is my living and calling? What do You mean, seven years?"

Of course, none of this made any sense until years later. During those seven years, my wife and I experienced so many trials in our preparation for ministry. I realize now that God was preparing me to be a prophetic voice. He intended those seven years to be a season when I was in a secret place with Him, one that would prepare me to receive His words mouth to mouth.

Those were the most difficult years of my life and ministry. Many times I wanted to die. I was fired twice and had to move out of our first little house we had bought when we were first married. We had setback after setback, hurt after hurt. I was often confused, not sure if I truly was called, but God was forming character and developing the gift. Looking back at those seven years, I thank God for that time. I believe it has helped me be a better person and minister.

The Lord did the same with many of His servants and prophets in Scripture. These seasons when God molds our character are not just limited to prophets, but God will place prophets in these seasons. God always took His prophets through many things, even putting them in hiding as He prepared them to be His spokesmen. He did this with Elijah, telling him, "Get away from here and turn eastward, and hide by the Brook Cherith, which flows into the Jordan" (1 Kings 17:3).

God put Elijah in hiding by telling him to go to the Brook Cherith, where he would be out of the public's eye. He was to hide there until the Lord brought him out. This is an important process for those the Lord raises up to be His spokesmen. We are to wait, allowing God to make us into the people He wants us to be, so He can develop our call. We must never forget that promotion comes from God. When God hides a prophet in the making, that person must learn to trust Him and the process. God was preparing Elijah to one day prophesy to King Ahab and Jezebel. He would have to stand alone with confidence and deliver words that were not going to make this king and queen very happy.

The local church may be *a secret place of hiding* where God prepares and trains His prophets today, just as the prophets in the local church at Antioch were trained there before they were later sent out to minister as an extension of the church. This is a point many miss in the prophetic. It is possible to have a legitimate gift—and even be called to be a prophet— yet bypass the hiding place of the local church.

There were three physical locations where Elisha went that represent his season of hiding. They hold some prophetic truths in understanding the making of a prophet. They were Cherith, Zarephath, and Beersheba.

- *Cherith* (1 Kings 17:3)—The meaning of the word *cherith* is a place or valley of dryness, or, in other words, the wilderness. This is where God humbles us, proves us, and sees what is in our hearts, just as He did when preparing the children of Israel to enter the Promised Land in Deuteronomy 8:2. Many great men of God received their preparation in a wilderness, including Elijah, Moses, John the Baptist, Jesus, and the apostle Paul. In this secret place of preparation, you may feel like you are in a wilderness where everything is dry and lifeless. Here you learn to prophesy to your destiny and to maintain your relationship with God regardless of how dry you feel. You learn how not to base your life on feeling but upon His promised destiny for you.

- *Zarephath* (1 Kings 17:9)—This place represents the place of fire and refining, where the Lord prepares you to be His prophetic spokesperson. The meaning for the word *zarephath* is the place of burning. In the process of God's refinement, we may feel that the heat of preparation is greater than we can bear. This is where many feel as though they have been forgotten. This is where God develops character. The prophet in this spiritual place learns how mercy triumphs over judgment. He learns humility and that he is not the only one who hears and speaks for God. There were seven thousand others in this experience with Elijah, even though he thought he was the only prophet around. God was purifying his gift.

- *Beersheba* (1 Kings 19:3–10)—In the Hebrew, this place means "the place of the well or pit." This is yet another place God uses to prepare His prophets. It was where Elijah faced things that were trying to discourage his calling. Elijah had to learn to overcome the feeling of loneliness and isolation. He dealt with rejection and feeling like he wanted to quit. Then he found himself in self-pity. This is often how the prophetic servant feels when hidden by God.

When God makes His prophets, He takes them through many of the examples we have seen from Elijah's life, so they learn to stand in the anointing of the olive tree of prophecy. To disrupt the process through unwillingness may only prolong it.

When God was taking me through the seven years of preparation, He wanted to develop godly character. The prophetic was very important in my life. Once when visiting a church, one of the worship team members of this church called me out and sang a prophetic song over me. The Lord spoke to me through this song and told me He hadn't forgotten me. He would not let me get off the path, and He told me He was calling me to a secret place in Him. This prophetic song said that if I would go to this place and time with God, I would one day see foreign lands. Today this prophecy has come to pass, as my wife and I travel around the world. I dare not think where I would be had I not come to the secret place to be hidden in Him!

This process may seem long, and at times you may feel like you are a failure. During my season of preparation, I had a vision. I saw someone I knew who was preaching and ministering to thousands as what appeared to be a golden-looking vessel. Then I saw myself in this same vision, broken into a million pieces on the ground. I looked like I was no good, and there was no hope. Suddenly the vision changed, and I was now standing up preaching as a golden vessel, while the person I had seen preaching at first was now broken in a million pieces.

Then the Lord told me, "Hank, you have allowed Me to break you so I can promote you, but that person allowed man to promote him, and so the devil will one day break him." That person had never gone through a time of preparation. The vision encouraged me to believe that one day I would make it OK because I was allowing God to break me of the things that were unpleasing to Him.

The Final Key

As we bring this chapter on God's gift of the prophet to closure, I want to give you a final key found in 2 Kings 4:8–10, once again from the story of Elisha and the Shunammite woman. After the prophet passed many times by the house of the Shunammite woman and her husband, she finally decided that she should make him a special room, a chamber, and give him a place to stay. Elisha agreed and received her offer. Her house was then joined to the prophetic.

Prophetically, the church needs to prepare a chamber for the prophets and the prophetic, not naturally speaking, but spiritually. In other words, it needs to *make room* for the prophetic. Then, in turn, prophets need to be willing to make their chamber—or abode—in the room prepared in the local church, just as Elisha did.

There are several things the Shunammite woman used in this story to make a room for the prophet. The things she provided in his room are things we must provide in our churches to make a place for the prophetic and those who have a prophetic calling.

- *The chamber*—The chamber is a place in which to dwell and find stability. When you have a chamber or room, you don't feel homeless. Making a room for the prophetic is providing an atmosphere that receives it and a place where God's prophetic people can be trained and equipped. It speaks of the local church receiving and providing a place to house or accommodate the prophetic ministry. In this way, the church can join itself to the prophetic.

- *A bed*—This is a place to pray and rest. This is where the prophet learns to hear the secrets of the Lord. It also speaks of submitting your gift to authority and resting so God can speak to you mouth to mouth. Prophets should feel welcome in our churches and not feel that their ministry is an inconvenience.

- *A table*—This is meant for maturing the believer in the meat of God's Word, not just milk that is meant for spiritual infants. This again speaks of having a place of feeding and growing to aid in your prophetic gifting. Churches should provide feeding and teaching to help prophets and prophetic people.

- *A stool*—This is a place of positioning one into a spiritual seat to reign in his or her gift with God's authority. This is a place to learn to function in your prophetic gift under proper authority. We are not a prophet to everyone and everything, and we will have to learn the boundaries of

our own authority. We must know how we are seated and
positioned in the authority God gives us.

- *The candlestick*—This is a place of revelation, which is
  available to those who will allow God to mold them in the
  prophetic. The candlestick gives light and insight by which
  we can read God's heart and receive revelation from Him.

These items were in the house of the Shunammite woman, and they
are items that are prophetically needed to enable prophets to rise up and
become the anointed gifts God wants them to be. They are not optional
but foundational. Prophets are anointed vessels that God has set into
the church, not to be a problem, but as a wonderful blessing. Let's allow
the operation of this wonderful gift. Whether you are called into the
prophet's office or you simply desire for God to use you to prophesy,
let me encourage you. If you will allow the Lord to prepare you, you
will surely be used in this anointing that is so dear to God's heart. Yes,
prophets are God's gifts, prepared and made by Him.

EIGHT

THE SECRET OF THE
WORD AND SPIRIT

For our gospel did not come to you in word only,
but also in power, and in the Holy Spirit.
–*1 Thessalonians 1:5*

T HE MUSIC QUIETED DOWN TO THE SOUND OF SOMEONE IN the congregation beginning to prophesy. I was visiting there with a minister friend who was the guest speaker. From the right side of the congregation, this person began to prophesy in a corrective tone about how the church needed to go back to the Word of God by walking in love and not focusing so much time on prophecy or the spiritual gifts. This prophecy mentioned that it was all about "the Word...the Word...the Word!"

The people on the right side began to shout and clap, giving their agreement to this word. Suddenly, as this person ended their prophecy, someone on the left side of the congregation began to prophesy more loudly and vocally than the one on the right. This prophecy corrected the church about focusing too much on the Word only and about walking in false love. This person continued in a corrective sort of prophecy and contradicted the first prophecy by saying it was now about the Spirit in this day, and this church needed to embrace the Spirit. The people who were on the left side began to clap and applaud this pathetic prophecy.

These two prophecies were about as contradictory as you could get. They were as divided as that church itself, even with different groups seated on opposite sides of the church!

I stood there listening, hardly believing what I was hearing. I shouldn't have been too surprised by it though, because earlier, before this meeting, my friend and I were praying together, and the Lord began to give me a spiritual vision of this church service. Neither one of us had ever attended there—and never went back. I had told my friend that I saw a person on the right side of the church begin to prophesy, holding his Bible and waving it in the air with a look of anger. Then I also saw in the vision a second person prophesying, but standing on the left, contradicting what the person on the right was saying. I told my friend, "It seems this church is divided over the Word of God and the Spirit of God."

What I had seen earlier was now being played out before us. It was apparent that some people felt they needed more preaching or focus on the Word of God, the Bible, with less emphasis on the gifts of the Spirit, as the prophecy suggested. It was also quite obvious that the other half of the church felt it was too Word of God–oriented at that church and some operations of the gifts of the Spirit were needed.

The truth of the matter was that this very divided church needed *both* the Word of God and the Spirit of God! They are both vital and necessary in the life of a church and should work together and agree.

THE SPIRIT AND THE WORD AGREE

We need a good balance of both the Word and the Spirit in our churches. We need the stability that the Word of God provides, but we need to add life and power through the manifestation of the Holy Spirit. The moves and manifestations of the Holy Spirit are what give life and confirm the truth of the Word preached. We can't have one without the other. If we have only the Word, we risk becoming dead, religious, and theological. But if we only have the Spirit, we create an environment of instability and disorder.

We also need both in the prophetic. We need the prophecy of Scripture, and we also need the prophecy that comes from the Spirit of God.

> Knowing this first, that no prophecy of Scripture is of any private interpretation, for prophecy never came by the will of man, but holy men of God spoke as they were moved by the Holy Spirit.
>
> —2 PETER 1:20-21

We see from this verse of Scripture that the Word of God and the Spirit work together in agreement. It is the Holy Spirit who inspired the written Word of God, and He is also the One who inspires prophecy. The highest form of prophecy is the written Word of God. In the Greek, it is referred to as the *logos*, which is the written Word. There is also the spirit of prophecy, or the present-day utterances of the Holy Spirit, which, in the Greek, is the word *rhema*. This refers to the spoken word.

It takes both the logos and the rhema word to hear and reveal the secrets of the Lord. Jesus said that man doesn't live by bread alone (Luke 4:4). This refers to not just natural bread but also to the supernatural bread of God's Word, the logos. In other words, we can't just have the written Word by itself. We also need every word that proceeds out of the mouth of God. This is rhema. The Word of God and the Spirit of God must work together or agree.

Just as the Word and Spirit partner together, we must partner with them if we are to be successful and fully inherit all God has for us. Our prophecies should always line up with the Scriptures. The Bible is the measuring stick of our prophetic words. As a person of the Word and Spirit, you can't be content only in the written prophecy of Scripture— the Word of God. You must also incorporate the supernatural present operation of the Holy Ghost. Even though the Word is the foundation of our Christian walk and is vitally important, we need to see the necessity of the moving of the Holy Spirit and prophecy.

Preaching the Word only, without emphasis on the Holy Spirit and His gifts, may result in churches and individuals who become lifeless, powerless, and void of the manifestations of the Holy Spirit. I heard a man say it this way years ago: "With only the Word, you will dry up, but with only the Spirit, you will blow up!" If we have the Spirit only and no strong biblical foundation or correct doctrine of the Word of God, we are out of balance. It takes both.

> Dishonest scales are an abomination to the LORD, but
> a just weight is His delight.
> —PROVERBS 11:1

A just weight of the Word and the Spirit is the Lord's delight, and we need a healthy balance of the two. They work together as a powerful tool. Shouting, dancing, and even prophesying, and having the Holy Ghost manifestations of the gifts are great. There is nothing wrong with these as long as we also give the Word of God equal importance.

However, I believe we are in a very dangerous, crucial time in the body of Christ today. If we don't begin to have Spirit-filled experiences in our churches along with a proper diet of the Word, then this generation may only read of past spiritual experiences and never experience them for themselves. Too often the Scriptures are preached with no power of the Holy Ghost to accompany it. When this is the case, we can become religious, traditional, stiff, and predictable, with little to no move of the Holy Spirit whatsoever. The Word without God's power can then become just the enticing words of man's wisdom without any demonstration of His power.

And my speech and my preaching were not with persuasive words of human wisdom, but in demonstration of the Spirit and of power.

—1 CORINTHIANS 2:4

It becomes what I call "John the Baptist type of Christianity"—where the Word is preached without any demonstration of power. John the Baptist preached the kingdom of God, but he did so without any demonstration of miracles. His one purpose was to put an emphasis on and draw attention to the Word, Jesus Christ. John was all about the Word: "Then many came to Him and said, 'John performed no sign, but all the things that John spoke about this Man were true'" (John 10:41). We never want to become caught up in the Word without the demonstration of power.

However, on the other hand, if our church services are only based on Holy Ghost manifestations without the teaching and feeding of the Word of God, we risk raising up a generation of unstable and undisciplined believers who will struggle to live by faith, especially when the day grows darker. In Luke 18:8, Jesus asked the question, "When the Son of Man comes, will He really find faith on the earth?" There is still only one primary way that faith is developed in our lives, and that is by feeding on God's Word, the Bible (Romans 10:17).

So today we have to ask ourselves, "Will the Son of God find faith on the earth?" Will His sheep be fed and taught the precious words of Scripture to mature them? Or will they yield to a spiritual manifestation movement without knowing how to use their faith? Will they believe God's Word and submit to proper biblical doctrine and application for their Christian lives?

To minister in the Spirit, however, without the Word of God can cause us to lose a level of our authority and power. Eventually, it becomes empty noise. Over time, the doctrine preached in these groups loses its edge of accuracy and gets shaky. Unfortunately, in some churches, the Word no longer has equal prominence as Holy Ghost manifestations and prophecy. Yet in others, the Spirit, unfortunately, doesn't have equal prominence as the Word being preached. Unless the Spirit and the Word are equally valued and important, balance is lacking. In the early church, the Spirit and the Word worked together. People were saved, matured, and grounded through the Word preached, but they also experienced powerful Holy Ghost miracles and wonders!

> And they went out and preached everywhere, the Lord working with them and confirming the word through the accompanying signs.
>
> —MARK 16:20

Notice that the preaching of the Word of God and the person of the Holy Ghost worked together with powerful results.

When it comes to the secrets of the Lord that we receive and minister to others, they must line up with the Word of God. To be an effective minister of the secrets of God, we must be students of the Word of God and vessels of the Spirit of God. "For our gospel did not come to you in word only, but also in power, and in the Holy Spirit" (1 Thessalonians 1:5).

There are many biblical examples of the Word of God and the Spirit of God working together. Here are a few:

- In the beginning was the Word, and the Word was with God, and the Word was God (Word) (John 1:1). In the beginning, the Spirit of God was hovering over the face of the waters (Spirit) (Genesis 1:1–2).

- Moses carried the Ten Commandments (Word) in his hand, and his face shown with the glory of God (Spirit) (Exodus 34:29).

- The valley of dry bones came to life by the word of Ezekiel (Word), and breath (Spirit) was prophesied into them (Ezekiel 37).

- There were two who witnessed the dedication of Jesus as a child: Simeon, whose name means to hear the word (Word), and Anna, whose name means grace, which is also where we derive the Greek word *charisma*, which is grace gifts (Spirit) (Luke 2).

- Jesus was transfigured with Moses standing by Him representing the Law (Word) and Elijah the prophet representing the prophetic (Spirit) (Matthew 17).

- Jesus's baptism and start of His ministry—Jesus was the Word that became flesh, and as He was baptized, a dove (Spirit) descended upon Him (Luke 3:21–22).

- In the church of Antioch, there were teachers (Word) and prophets (Spirit) working together (Acts 13:1).

- When Paul preached (Word), the Holy Ghost fell, baptizing the people in the Holy Ghost (Spirit) (Acts 11:15; 19).

The more we balance our Christian life with God's Word and His Spirit, the more grounded we will be as Christians who operate in His power in awesome ways and touch people's lives.

MARS HILL PROPHETIC

When the Word and Spirit are not correctly balanced in our lives, we can get out of order. The Word and Spirit working together create a strong, well-balanced, healthy prophetic atmosphere. But when one or the other is missing or overemphasized, we can become out of balance. The apostle Paul had to confront such imbalance in Athens at a place called Mars Hill.

> For all the Athenians and the foreigners who were there spent their time in nothing else but either to tell or to hear some new thing. Then Paul stood in the midst

of the Areopagus and said, "Men of Athens, I perceive
that in all things you are very religious."

—Acts 17:21-22

The people in Athens always wanted to hear, see, or experience some
new thing. Eventually they became spiritually superstitious or acted
overly spiritual. We know these people at Athens were unsaved, but this
points to the same kind of behavior regarding things of the Spirit among
some in the prophetic. Without a balance of the Word of God and the
Spirit of God, we can become spiritually out of order. It is one thing
when you desire to see and hear fresh things from the Lord. It is another
thing when we idolize it so much that, like these on Mars Hill, we do
nothing but go from meeting to meeting and manifestation to manifestation in search of some new thing. We cease to care about hearing
sound preaching, which will change our character. I am certainly not
implying we shouldn't hunger and desire for the biblical manifestations
of the Holy Spirit and partake of meetings where such is happening. We
should desire for God to speak and show us things this way. However, a
Mars Hill type of prophetic is the addiction to always hear or see some
new thing, which leads to the spiritually superstitious belief that everything is prophetic or supernatural. This leads to spiritual weirdness and
lack of true biblical stability.

This is especially true if what we are seeing and hearing doesn't line
up with Scripture or correct doctrine. To avoid the Mars Hill prophetic
syndrome, we should avoid only being led by prophets or prophecy, even
though God will speak through them concerning our future destiny.
The first place we go to hear from God should be to the Word of God.
The prophetic words we receive should be judged for correctness and
tested by God's Word. Learn to be rooted and grounded in God's Word
before you start running all over to hear and see some *new thing* or some
new "wind of doctrine" (Ephesians 4:14).

Some live from hype to hype and manifestation to manifestation.
They go from church to church, meeting to meeting, always looking for

the greatest show on earth. Our prophetic gatherings shouldn't become a prophetic circus of seeing and hearing some new show. We must be like those in the prophetic who correctly use their gatherings as opportunities to teach the Word of God and equip the believers to do the work of the ministry. They teach people how to flow in the prophetic and things of the Holy Spirit correctly. But they also emphasize the importance of being connected to a local church and to a pastor who preaches sound doctrine from the Bible.

To be free from this Mars Hills syndrome, one must be grounded in the Word of God while continuing to desire the Spirit of God. Be sure that you are being grounded and rooted in a good local church and that you are learning the things of the Word of God as well as the Spirit of God. The Bible should always be your foundation and measuring stick to judge what you see and hear—not the other way around. You don't measure the Word by your spiritual experiences or the prophetic.

Don't become like those who use the prophetic word to determine what they want to live by and agree with. These people are always seeking new words and feel that gives them license to sidestep the Bible. They look for a better word than the last one they received, as an addict looks for the next fix. They have withdrawals if they don't see it, hear it, or have some new moment.

Yes, we should covet earnestly the gifts and manifestations of the Spirit. There have been times in my life when I have received a prophetic word from the Lord in different meetings I went to or from a prophetic ministry through which God spoke to me. But although they were a great blessing to me, I didn't depend on that word over my Bible reading time with God or my study of the Word of God and my service in the church I attended.

Jesus gave a word to His disciples when He told them to get in their boat and go to the other side (Mark 4:35). This word carried them until a great storm came and they thought they were going to perish. Jesus was sound asleep in the boat, and after waking Him, they wanted a new word to carry them through their unknown storm rather than to hold on to the word that the Lord gave them earlier. This is exactly what Mars Hills prophetic does. It doesn't hold on to the Word of the Lord. It keeps seeking for something greater and more spectacular to carry the person through life.

I have known people who live from prophecy to prophecy, wanting me to prophesy the next exciting thing. When it looks like one prophetic word they receive isn't coming to pass the way they expected, they want you to prophesy a new word to keep them going.

When referring to John the Baptist's prophetic ministry, Jesus said, "What did you go out into the wilderness to see? A reed shaken by the wind?" (Luke 7:24). A prophet's ministry and the prophetic can gather many who want to hear the word of the Lord or to see something super-natural. However, we must not get into a performance-based mind-set, whether we are the one delivering the secrets of the Lord or just coming to receive. This can make us do things that the Holy Ghost did not command or endorse. The Word and Spirit must work together. The Word should be preached, and the Holy Spirit should be allowed to demonstrate His gifts and power in line with that Word.

I have ministered in meetings where all God wanted me to do was to preach the Word, close my Bible, and end the meeting. Then I have had other meetings where I carefully prepared a message from Scripture, but the manifestations of the Holy Ghost took over with miracles and the prophetic.

A group of ladies were sitting in the congregation of one meeting where I was ministering, *expecting* me to prophesy. I have no problem with expectant faith, but I do have a problem when someone tries to pull the preacher into whatever that person wants to hear. Well, these ladies were pulling so hard that I knew they only came to see me prophesy. I could feel it. You could tell by their body language and responses that they didn't come to hear me preach. They wanted me to stop and prophesy to them.

However, I had specific instructions from the Lord that night. I felt I was only to preach the Word of God, because that church did not need to hear the prophetic message through prophecy but from God's Word. I didn't like the spirit I felt from that group of women visiting. I sensed that they were undisciplined and not under the authority of a pastor. Their mannerisms were drawing attention to themselves. Their behavior or spirit didn't sit well with me. In obedience to what I felt from the Lord, I didn't minister prophetically other than through my preaching. I taught out of the Bible and ended the service with a prayer. Those women were mad, and I knew it, but I was very happy that I didn't perform for them and get off of what the Lord spoke to me earlier.

After the service, some pastors and leaders from around the region who were in the service couldn't stop thanking me. These were leaders who loved and welcomed the prophetic in their churches, but they knew that the Word from Scripture was exactly what had been needed in that meeting. They knew that group of ladies had been the cause of many problems around the area, claiming to have great prophetic insight. In fact, some of the leaders said these women had even caused church splits. They were not submitted to a pastor, and their prophetic input was always out of order.

I was glad I didn't get caught up in performance and pride. I wasn't about to let these ladies cause that meeting to be a *Mars Hill* experience to their satisfaction.

We need to be people of the Word and Spirit. We must teach people the Word of God, feed them, and build them up. Then we must allow the Holy Spirit to come and manifest in the gifts as well. Neither the Word nor the Spirit should be overemphasized. We need the balance of both and should be disciplined to follow the Lord's plans and not just do things to do them.

Learning to be disciplined, mature, mannerly, and well versed in the Scriptures will help people appreciate the prophetic as they see us be people who love both God's Word and the Holy Spirit.

Good for Us—and Good for the Holy Ghost

There is a principle in Acts 15:28 that will keep us from performing in the flesh. This same principle will help us to step out in the prophetic correctly and to avoid mishandling the prophetic. In Acts 15:28 we read, "For it seemed good to the Holy Spirit, and to us."

Paul and his team acted first upon what they felt they received from the Lord, desiring to minister what the Holy Spirit wanted them to minister. They weren't out for what they wanted. Doing this will keep a Mars Hill prophetic spirit from dominating you.

It is evident that they were working in partnership with the Holy Spirit. They didn't just step out on their own and assert, "After all, we are a prophetic people, and we can prophesy whenever we want!" This isn't meant to imply that the only time you step out to prophesy is when you have to have a special feeling or goose pimple. It is meant to remind us of the importance of working with the Holy Spirit as our partner and of being sensitive to His voice and leading—not just doing things because we can.

The Lord wants us to prophesy and stir up our prophetic spirit regularly. However, sometimes we can be so quick to speak that we don't wait to see if it is good for the Holy Ghost. We aren't careful to wait to hear His voice or instruction. We must learn to be sensitive to the will of the Holy Spirit. Something might seem good to us but may not be good for the Holy Ghost.

In some cases, He may tell us to be silent. There have been times when the Lord stopped me from giving someone a word, even going so far as to remind me that the person needed to obey and act on the other words he or she had already received. At other times we may need to wait for more clarity about what the Spirit is saying. Then there are definitely times when we need to just open our mouth in faith and let the words come out!

In the days of the early church, the people relied on the Holy Ghost in all that they did. Consider these following examples:

He [Jesus] through the Holy Spirit had given commandments to the apostles.

—Acts 1:2

You always resist the Holy Spirit; as your fathers did,
so do you.

—Acts 7:51

As they ministered to the Lord and fasted, the Holy
Spirit said...

—Acts 13:2

So, being sent out by the Holy Spirit...

—Acts 13:4

It seemed good to the Holy Spirit, and to us.

—Acts 15:28

They were forbidden by the Holy Spirit to preach the
word in Asia.

—Acts 16:6

The Holy Spirit testifies in every city.

—Acts 20:23

Thus says the Holy Spirit...

—Acts 21:11

In the example in Acts 16:6, they were forbidden of the Holy Spirit
to preach in Asia. I believe if the Holy Spirit forbade them to do that,
there are times when He will forbid us to do certain things when it
comes to ministering in the gifts. We must become more disciplined to
minister with the Holy Ghost and be led by Him. We can't just speak
and prophesy so freely and call it *being led*. Just because the prophecy
carries a degree of accuracy doesn't mean the Spirit wants it spoken at

that moment! Discipline yourself to listen to the Holy Spirit. It will increase your measure of authority and help you know the difference.

This is why the prophet Elijah heard the still, small voice of God, which wasn't found in the wind, earthquake, or fire. God was teaching him to listen for that still, small voice of God and sense His leadings. Yes, the Holy Spirit is waiting to manifest Himself to others. However, there are times when He will tell you to be silent, hold off, or do something else besides prophesy.

There are many times when even though you won't feel a thing, God will move through you. I was once asked to minister to a businessman I had never met while at a barbecue. I didn't feel like prophesying or even hearing what God might be saying. The pastor of the church insisted, telling me how important this was, so I agreed. I didn't feel any special feeling or leading of the Holy Ghost, nor did I sense the Holy Ghost stopping me. Instead, I had just the insistence of the pastor. Typically, when I am at a social event, I don't like being put on the spot to minister the word of the Lord. I began to tell the businessman some things I felt, naming specific incidences and cities he was involved in. He was very blessed and touched by the word I gave him. I didn't know him, and my mind was on eating, but I was able to tap into the grace that was already upon me. We need to stay full of His Word and His Spirit and be ready in season and out of season. However, any time when I feel that God the Holy Ghost does not want me to say something, I do not say a word.

Sometimes the Holy Ghost wants to speak and is waiting for us to step out in faith. Smith Wigglesworth once said, "If the Spirit doesn't move, then I will move the Spirit!" The history of this man's life is unmatched today in many ways because he learned how to tap into the grace inside him.

At other times, we need to be sensitive to His will and His desires and wait to see what the Lord wants. We can't have just one style when it comes to the prophetic. An example of waiting on the Holy Spirit can be found in Luke 4:25–27, where we learn that there were many lepers in Israel, but the prophet Elijah was sent by the Spirit *to only one.* It wasn't to many; it was to only one! He didn't start gathering the widows of Israel and start holding prophetic nights for them. That doesn't mean we don't or can't hold prophetic nights. We just need to be open to the Holy Spirit's direction and instruction, which may lead us in a different direction. Elijah was on a specific task and spiritual assignment. He was led by the Spirit of God to one, not all, and he didn't speak and minister to everyone.

We need to be led by the Spirit and filled with Him so we are ready to tap into that grace and minister to others. Some people have suggested that you can never speak the secrets of God unless moved upon by the Spirit, while others suggest you can do it anytime at will. I believe both are correct and have their place, depending on the factors involved. We must learn prophetic assignments and the leading of the Holy Ghost.

If we don't learn to be led of the Holy Spirit, we risk learning to be led by men, often like a dog on a leash at the control and hand of someone else. Whenever they want you to prophesy and *turn on the juice*, that is what you do. This is not wise. There is a time to speak and a time to be silent. There are prophets of the Lord and prophets of the land. We must be open to difficult prophetic operations and plans of the Holy Spirit. Prophets of the Lord speak for God and learn the discipline of waiting for directives from the Lord to speak what He says. Prophets of the land will speak what man wants to hear, often without consulting with the Lord on the matter. You have to stay where the Lord wants you.

STAY IN YOUR REALM OF AUTHORITY

Those who are called to function in the prophet's office must learn to stay in their field of authority. For example, the apostle Paul mentioned that he was not an apostle to everyone. He even stated that he wouldn't boast beyond his measure of authority (2 Corinthians 10:13). He knew his spiritual authority and calling, and he knew his limits. We see an example of God's limits in Revelation 11:1–2:

I was given a stick for a measuring rod and told, "Get up and measure God's Temple and Altar and everyone worshiping in it. Exclude the outside court; don't measure it."

—THE MESSAGE

This verse speaks of prophetic discernment and the realm of authority. John was given a rod of authority to measure everything except the outside court. He wasn't given a rod of authority to measure there. This is true today for us. We aren't called to be a prophet to everyone, every nation, every city, or every church. Our measure of rule, grace, and authority is given to us by Jesus. We aren't to go beyond the measure given and that was confirmed by the leadership of the local church. This will help us minister what is good unto the Holy Ghost.

If all we do is minister that which is good to us and not to the Holy Ghost, we may prophesy from our soul, not our spirit. In Ezekiel 3:1–4, a prophetic example is given of ministering from our spirit and not from our head or emotions. Ezekiel was to eat the scroll, which was the Word of the Lord, and get it in his belly, which was his spirit. It was after he got this word in his belly that he was to share it. In other words, the prophetic word he received from the Lord had to get into his spirit so that it would be released from his spirit, bypassing his head, his emotions, and his flesh. This kept it from being Ezekiel's words, and ensured that what he said was from the Lord.

At times I have allowed my soul and familiarity to get in the way of my ability to hear the secrets of God. The tendency can be to keep ministering more and more words to the same individual out of your emotions rather than your spirit. Jesus said, "He who believes in Me, as the Scripture has said, out of his heart will flow rivers of living water" (John 7:38). The secrets of the Lord should come from the Spirit of God into our spirits—Spirit to spirit, or mouth to mouth.

Sometimes the one receiving and ministering the secrets can get caught up in his or her own emotions and not hear or speak the prophetic word correctly. How, then, do we know if something is spoken from the flesh (soul) or from the spirit? We need to be able to recognize the difference between genuine manifestations of the Holy Spirit and when something is of the flesh or, in rare cases, even from a demonic spirit. Even in the ministry of Jesus there were people who acted out in their soul or flesh. In some cases, the devil even manifested.

In Luke 9:52–55, James and John wanted to call down a supernatural fire on the Samaritans who didn't receive the Lord. Jesus told His disciples that they were in the flesh. He said, "You do not know what manner of spirit you are of" (verse 55). The disciples were unable to discern that they were operating from the flesh.

When the gifts of the Spirit are being manifested, sometimes undisciplined people will get into the flesh and make mistakes. We shouldn't live in fear of that, especially when a good leader or pastor is governing the setting. We certainly don't want to eliminate true supernatural manifestations just because of a few who make mistakes, usually with good intentions. A certain number of mistakes are acceptable. Everyone has stepped out in the flesh before, even the most seasoned generals in the faith! While we need to be discerning and strive for the truth, we can't become so fearful, critical, and nitpicky that no one is able to forge new ground, grow in prophecy, or learn to flow in the Spirit.

Rarely will you encounter a serious demonic manifestation by someone trying to deliver a "gift of the Spirit." To help us know the difference between genuine manifestations and the flesh, here are five helpful guidelines:

1. *Did it give you or others a good feeling overall?* While we can all have uncertain feelings about the unfamiliar (recall the first time you heard speaking in tongues), a very heavy feeling may reveal that something is off. It is like a warning or red light.

2. *Is the person ministering proven?* If the person operating in the Spirit is committed to a solid church and is a stable Christian or a proven minister, then give that person some consideration.

3. *Were you or the person receiving blessed?* If something good came from it, then it is probably from the Lord. Even if the immediate response by the recipient wasn't too positive, decide if the ministry truly helped that person. Did fruit result from the ministry?

4. *Was it biblical overall?* Not every expression of the Spirit is detailed in the Bible because they are too numerous to contain in one book (John 21:25). However, all manifestations should agree with Bible doctrine. Was it orderly, in love, full of faith, in truth, and pure?

5. *Be like the Bereans* (Acts 17:11). First, they were joyful and receptive, and second, they followed up with study to confirm and strengthen what they received. Often we criticize first and then rarely give it any serious study afterward because of our predetermined opinions.

These principles will help you to be solid in the Word and the Spirit.

LIFE, LIGHT, AND POWER

This grace in us is given when we are born again and filled with His Spirit. When we are born again and Spirit filled, we receive life, light, and power. This life, light, and power are already in us and help us to tap into the gifts of the Spirit by faith. Life, light, and power are the very fabric woven into every believer who is born again and filled with His Holy Spirit. This means that every believer has the ability to flow in the gifts of the Spirit by what he or she already possesses through salvation and the baptism of the Holy Spirit. In us are the *life* of the Father, the *light* of Jesus, and the *power* of His Holy Spirit!

Jesus is the life that brought light to all mankind, but that life comes from the heavenly Father. John 1:4 says, "In Him was life, and the life was the light of men." When you were born again, Jesus *remade* you into a new creature so you would be able to receive this new life from the Father. Jesus came to Earth with the life of His heavenly Father inside Him so He could give that life to you. Jesus told us that He came to give us life more abundantly (John 10:10). This new life from the Father is placed inside of us through the person of the Holy Spirit (John 4:6, 26; 5:26; 2 Corinthians 5:2; Galatians 2:20).

Jesus produced life in us at the time of salvation, but that life produced something else in us called *light*. Jesus is the light, and He lights all men who receive Him. In Christ, we are the light of the world and should let our light shine before all men (John 1:4, 9).

> I am the light of the world. He who follows Me shall
> not walk in darkness, but have the light of life.
> —JOHN 8:12

Jesus gave us life and light. He also said that we would receive power after the Holy Ghost came upon us and we would be His witnesses (Acts 1:8). We become His witnesses when we display His power and gifts to people. The Holy Spirit is the One who activates the power of God in the earth, and He does it through us. These elements of life, light, and power were imparted to us when we were saved and filled with the Holy Spirit.

These three elements also coincide with the nine gifts of the Spirit. The gifts of the Spirit can be divided into three categories, which relate to life, light, and power. You can think of the gifts of the Spirit as the tools of the Holy Spirit, which draw the life, light, and power out of us. The gifts of the Spirit can be divided into three categories as follows according to 1 Corinthians 12:8–10:

- *The vocal gifts*—prophecy, different kinds of tongues, and the interpretation of tongues
- *The revelation gifts*—word of wisdom, word of knowledge, and discerning of spirits
- *The power gifts*—healing, faith, and working miracles

The vocal gifts produce *life*

"Death and life are in the power of the tongue" (Proverbs 18:21). When you speak under the power of the Holy Spirit from your mouth, it will produce and bring forth life. Since the vocal, also referred to as *utterance gifts*, are spoken words, we can see that they have the power to produce life.

The revelation gifts produce *light*

"That the God of our Lord Jesus Christ, the Father of glory, may give to you the spirit of wisdom and revelation in the knowledge of Him" (Ephesians 1:17). Revelation is light. Have you heard the expression "A light just went off in my head"? People say it when they suddenly get a revelation of something. The three revelation gifts bring light to people and situations because they reveal things to them they didn't know previously.

The power gifts produce *power*

"You shall receive power when the Holy Spirit has come upon you" (Acts 1:8). The power gifts are just that—they produce the manifested power of the God who lives inside you. God gives these gifts of His Spirit to show His glory through miracles, signs, and wonders.

Life, light, and power are already in us. To tap into these three, one must understand the connection between the infilling of the Holy Spirit and prophecy. Life, light, and power flow forth through the gifts of the Spirit when someone is filled with the Holy Ghost. The more a person prays in the Spirit, the more the flow of life, light, and power will manifest through the gifts.

THE HOLY GHOST BAPTISM AND GOD'S SECRETS

When Jesus, who was full of life, light, and power, was baptized, the Bible says He was filled with the Holy Ghost and a dove came and settled upon Him. Immediately, a prophetic voice came from heaven and said, "This is My beloved Son, in whom I am well pleased" (Matthew 3:17). The dove and a prophetic spoken word occurred at the same time. In the same way, the baptism of the Holy Ghost and prophecy work together to bring the secrets of God into manifestation. This is a key principle to keeping a powerful flow of the prophetic in our lives.

> And when Paul had laid hands on them, the Holy
> Spirit came upon them, and they spoke with tongues
> and prophesied.
>
> —ACTS 19:6

When they were filled with the Holy Spirit in this verse, they spoke in tongues, and they also prophesied. One of the key ways to tap into the grace inside you is by praying in the Holy Ghost. This makes us sensitive to the voice of the Lord and His secrets. The Holy Ghost and prophecy work together. The more we pray in the Spirit, the easier it is to tap into the grace that is in us, and the more the secrets of God will increase.

There are biblical examples to show how being filled with the Holy Spirit and the secrets of the Lord work together:

> And Elizabeth was filled with the Holy Spirit. Then she
> spoke out with a loud voice and said, "Blessed are you
> among women, and blessed is the fruit of your womb!"
>
> —LUKE 1:41–42

Now his father Zacharias was filled with the Holy Spirit, and prophesied.

—Luke 1:67

And they were all filled with the Holy Spirit and began to speak with other tongues, as the Spirit gave them utterance.

—Acts 2:4

And it shall come to pass in the last days, says God, that I will pour out of My Spirit on all flesh; your sons and your daughters shall prophesy.

—Acts 2:17

And when Paul had laid hands on them, the Holy Spirit came upon them, and they spoke with tongues and prophesied.

—Acts 19:6

All of these scriptural examples show us a divine connection between being filled with the Holy Ghost and prophecy. Praying and fellowshiping in the Holy Spirit will help us prophesy the Lord's secrets more easily and more accurately.

Paul said that when we pray in tongues, we are to pray that we may interpret those tongues (1 Corinthians 14:13). This doesn't mean the only time you can pray in tongues is if it is interpreted. This verse was especially true in a public church setting where God was giving a message in tongues to the congregation that required an interpretation, not necessarily when the believer is praying to God in tongues. Jesus showed this prophetically when He filled up the water pots in His first miracle of turning water to wine (John 2:1–11). This entire miracle was a picture of the coming infilling of the new wine of the Holy Spirit. In fact, on the Day of Pentecost, the onlookers thought the disciples were full of new wine!

After telling them to fill the water pots, Jesus instructed them to draw out of it. I believe this is representative of interpreting your tongues. In other words, you draw out the new wine of the Spirit that is created inside you when you pray in the Spirit. Then, just as they did when Jesus turned the water to wine, you can serve it to others.

BREAK OPEN THE FOUNTAIN OF YOUR DEEP

Drawing out of your spirit is literally being able to draw from the things the Holy Spirit has put inside you. However, sometimes you have to break it open to get the flow started. Look at Genesis 7:11: "On that day all the fountains of the great deep were broken up, and the windows of heaven were opened." Just as God released His power when the flood-waters of Noah's day were loosed, you can break open the deep things of God in your spirit by praying in the Spirit. Praying in the Spirit will cause the rivers of God's prophetic to flow out of you into the lives of others with great power. It helps you tap into the life, light, and power that is in you, which helps you discern what is good unto the Holy Ghost. You break open the fountain and draw out the new wine of the Spirit inside.

This is how we stir up the gifts of God. The apostle Paul told his young spiritual son Timothy to stir up the gift of God that was given to him by the laying on of hands and prophecy (2 Timothy 1:6). We stir our spirit to receive what God is giving to us by mouth-to-mouth transmission. The secrets of the Lord start coming from the depth of our spirit when we pray in the Spirit. Then when we open our mouths to speak by the Holy Ghost, the anointing and the secrets of the Lord will flow.

My wife, Brenda, and I often demonstrate this operation of the Holy Ghost and prophecy in our meetings through tongues and interpretation of tongues. The Lord will often speak a prophetic tongue through me, and my wife will interpret it over either individuals or churches.

When we continually draw the new wine out of our spirit by

breaking open the fountain of our deep, we stay in a constant place of readiness to minister by the Holy Ghost. Look here at some of the biblical results of breaking open the fountain of our deep by praying in the Holy Ghost and speaking out His prophetic secrets, as found in Genesis 7:18–20, 24:

> The waters prevailed and greatly increased on the earth....And the waters prevailed exceedingly on the earth...fifteen cubits upward....And the waters prevailed on the earth one hundred and fifty days.

In all of these examples, notice how the waters prevailed. Why? This is because when you pray in the Spirit, breaking open the fountain of your deep, you will prevail! You don't have to figure it out in your head; you just allow the anointing to come from the heart. Have you ever noticed the difference between a child and adult when they receive a gift? The child will just rip it open, while an adult often has to examine it and figure it out. Adults will usually say things like, "Oh, you shouldn't have!" This is exactly what happens when it comes to operating in the secrets of God. Rather than come like a child and tap into the gift by faith, we act skeptical and, at times, even unworthy. It hinders us from tapping into the fountain of our deep.

Another way that the Holy Spirit aids us in receiving accurate secrets from the Lord is by simply asking the Holy Spirit what is on His heart. Talk to Him, and listen to His voice. It will change your life. Rather than just rattling off a prayer list, ask Him what is important to Him. You will be surprised what you hear when you take time to ask Him. Setting time aside to fellowship with the Holy Spirit is important, and He loves it when you do. Coupled with praying in the Spirit, it will create a greater awareness to the prophetic voice of the Spirit.

As you can probably see by now, it is the checks and balances that we have covered in this chapter that will make you well rounded in the prophetic. As we follow the Holy Spirit and stay grounded in the

Word of God, we will draw out the new wine of God's Spirit from the depths of our spirit. Then, as God's secrets come forth, it will be a beautiful picture of the Word and the Spirit operating together as a powerful team.

NINE

ALIGNING YOURSELF WITH THE PROPHETIC WORD

Timothy, my son, I give you this instruction in
keeping with the prophecies once made about you, so
that by following them you may fight the good fight,
holding on to faith and a good conscience. Some have
rejected these and so have shipwrecked their faith.

–1 Timothy 1:18–19, NIV

WHILE MINISTERING, I KEPT SENSING THE LORD SPEAKING A secret to me. I was hearing a month and a day, and I felt in my heart it was referring to someone's birthday. What I didn't know was that the person with a birthday was a backslidden Christian. She was invited to the meeting and hesitated to go, and she wasn't quite sure of the prophetic demonstrations of the Holy Spirit. She prayed privately, saying, "God, if all this prophetic stuff is legitimate, then have this preacher call out my birthday." Unaware of this person's request, I was now speaking the exact month and day of her birthday. She was shocked, to say the least.

The Lord went on to reveal that a ball and chain was connected to her feet, spiritually speaking. Then I began to give a prophetic demonstration by imitating someone walking bound to a ball and chain. I walked down the center aisle of the church and spoke to her of someone she was dating who lived in a different state. I told her that God was looking at certain choices in her life and decisions concerning this relationship.

I chose my words carefully so as not to reveal the situation to the congregation. I never want to embarrass anyone by giving too many personal details about a life. This person I prophesied to started to cry, knowing that this was a true word from the Lord. The critical key in this story is the fact that she immediately aligned herself correctly with what the Lord was telling her, and she knew exactly what she needed to do. She broke the ball and chain off by breaking off this dating relationship. Hearing this secret from God proved to be a blessing, but it was conditional upon the proper response from her. Thank God she did what was necessary. Today she is happily married to someone other than the person she was dating at that time.

They contacted our ministry later to let me know that they are in ministry today, and God is using them powerfully. Aligning herself with the word of the Lord changed her life. I didn't tell her what to do; I just reported what God was saying in a way that she knew it was the Lord speaking. The prophetic secret God spoke was dependent upon her actions and obedience.

Secrets revealed from the Lord are meant to be a blessing when we choose to align ourselves with them. When God speaks a word such as the one I just talked about, God wants lasting fruit to be produced in our lives. You may be thinking, "Yes, I want to align myself with God's prophetic word, but with what I am facing right now, I just need a secret from God to align with!" There are different kinds of prophetic secrets or words that God has for us, and there are different conditions that go with them.

Different Kinds of Secrets

We must never forget that God is for us. Some people believe that in theory but are not so confident to believe it to the point that they actually hear God speaking a good word in their life. But God has come to give us hope and a future (Jeremiah 29:11), and He does this through prophetic secrets. Secrets, when they are revealed from God, can bring decreed blessings, prophetic announcements, prophetic directions, prophetic warnings, and prophetic revelations. Throughout Scripture, we see many examples of these prophetic words, which were given expressly to change people's lives for good.

I would like to share some examples of different kinds of prophetic secrets in the Bible coupled with personal examples. The purpose is to draw attention to how God uses the prophetic word to save and change lives. When we align with it, we will bear eternal fruit. I want to show you how prophetic secrets worked in Bible days and also how they work and help us today.

Prophetic blessings

The first example is when God decrees prophetic blessings. In Scripture, blessings were often decreed over individuals to pronounce blessings over their lives and future. This is especially true with many fathers in the Bible. Before many of these patriarchs departed from the earth, they revealed the secrets of the Lord to their children, pronouncing blessing and revealing the prophetic plan of God for their future. At other times, when children were born, fathers decreed a prophetic blessing over the infant. This prophetic blessing was so important that a mother named Rebekah and her son Jacob deceived his father, Isaac, and twin brother, Esau, into giving the father's blessing to Jacob. This decree of blessing was so important to Rebekah and Jacob that they were willing to steal it deceitfully away from Esau (Genesis 27).

One of the most powerful and necessary things parents can do today is pronounce prophetic blessings over their children's lives. You can do it as you are tucking your children into bed and speaking prophetic prayers and blessings over them during that time. You can pray prophetic scriptures over them during special times of prayer. These prophetic blessings are powerful and will bring the blessing of God into manifestation if you speak it and believe it. If you are a parent, or even if you are not, ask God to give you secrets from heaven to speak over your own life and over your children that will strategically bring God's blessing for your future and theirs.

When God created Adam, the first thing He did was bless him (Genesis 1:28). Do you know what that means? It literally means to say something good. God was pronouncing a prophetic blessing of good over Adam from the very first days of creation.

Prophetic words of blessing also brought comfort and gave hope in difficult situations. Jesus told the people gathered at the tomb of Lazarus that they were not to weep, because Lazarus wasn't actually dead—he only was sleeping. He declared the blessing of what was going to come to pass in God's plan before it happened. Jesus often spoke these blessings over people even when they weren't present. Remember the centurion's servant who was sick (Matthew 8:5–13)? Jesus declared a blessing over him even though he was at home.

I remember a time when God used my wife, Brenda, to speak a prophetic blessing over someone when the person wasn't present in the conference where she was ministering. The Lord had her call out a lady and tell her God knew she had come a long way to the conference and yet was feeling badly because she left her very sick child at home. She was concerned about leaving but had come to the meeting by faith anyway, trusting God for a miracle. What my wife didn't know was that this woman's tiny baby was in intensive care and needed a miracle. At that moment, my wife told her that her child was healed from that hour forward. When this woman arrived home, her child had already been taken off the ventilator and was healed, just as Brenda said while the mother was still at the conference. Her faith positioned her for a blessing and a miracle. This mother returned home to a healed baby. Thank God for the pronouncing of prophetic blessings!

Prophetic announcements

There were prophetic announcements that were revealed to individuals or groups of people. These announcements revealed secrets designed to prepare people for an upcoming event. We see this at the time of the birth of Jesus when the angel Gabriel came to Mary and told her the prophetic secret about the baby she was going to have.

A few years ago, the Lord gave me a prophetic announcement concerning the gas prices increasing. I believe God was preparing many in this nation for what was going to come. At the time I prophesied it, the gas prices were about a dollar something a gallon. This was years before the prices skyrocketed. The Lord revealed that they would reach four to five dollars a gallon and that we were to laugh at the oil prices as an act of faith. However, it was some time before the price of gas went up. God was giving an early announcement so we could pray, prepare, resist fear, and keep a joyful spirit while trusting Him.

Prophetic direction

The Lord also gave many prophetic secrets for the purpose of direction and instruction. These directions from God are secrets that give people specific tasks so that God can fulfill His purposes. Jesus gave an example of this when He told His disciples to go find a donkey that had never been ridden before. He was giving them instruction so they could help facilitate the prophetic event of His triumphant entry into Jerusalem.

I remember one time when God used me to give a prophetic direction that helped a pastor find the location to build a new church facility. The prophetic secret spoke the location and the amount of exact acres for the new building site. It helped this pastor locate the will of God.

He obeyed the prophetic direction, and, to God's glory, he has a new building today!

Prophetic warnings

There are also prophetic warnings that God uses to warn people of a potential catastrophe. The Lord will often give these warnings in order to divert a possible judgment or plot of the enemy. For example, the prophet Agabus gave a prophetic warning about a great famine that was coming (Acts 11:28). It was God's intent to prepare the people for this difficult time in history. Sometimes God will give these warnings so we can intercept something through prayer.

In the beginning of 2008, the Lord had me prophesy concerning that particular year in the United States. The Lord warned that it was a year to speak to the sky through prayer. He foretold that it would be a year of tornadoes and raging winds. We were to speak over our cities and our nation in order to stand against these winds and adverse weather patterns. The Lord was forewarning us so we could pray against them. In my own city of Omaha, we prayed because I had spoken this word more than once. God even spoke the month that we were to watch and pray for protection over our city.

While Omaha is considered part of the nation's tornado alley, the city itself had not experienced a direct touchdown of a serious, damaging tornado for more than thirty years. Yet it happened in the exact month the Lord had indicated. Two serious tornadoes hit, creating serious property damage. Throughout the same tornado season, we experienced more tornado activity and damage than we had in a long time. Thank God that the people prayed and lives were spared! These are just some personal examples of prophetic warnings.

Prophetic revelation

Finally, we know that the Lord also gave prophetic revelation to bring understanding, wisdom, and insight. This is so we understand what God is doing. Prophetic revelation gives us the ability to follow Him with clarity. Jesus gave prophetic revelation by explaining the plan of salvation through the Cross and Resurrection. He plainly told His disciples He would die and then rise again. He was trying to get them to understand through prophetic revelation what was about to happen so they could respond to God's plan. Prophetic revelation will also help you relate natural events to spiritual issues.

The Lord gave me a unique prophetic revelation that there would be unusual occurrences of snow that fell in 2007 and the early part of 2008. He prophesied that it would snow not only in places that it normally didn't snow but also in places that it did snow—but with record snowfall totals. The Lord placed attention on the Ohio Valley and New England states. The purpose of this prophetic revelation was to reveal the prophetic purpose of the Lord for those places. It spoke specifically of a prophetic sign of cleansing. Snow often represents spiritual cleansing, and the Lord was using snow to show His prophetic plan to create change in those areas.

It happened just as the Lord revealed, snowing in some very unusual places. I want to show you some of the places where snow was documented during those two years, and I am sure you will easily be able to see that God wants to work a spiritual cleansing in these locations.

The prophecy of unusual snow was given nationally on September 24, 2007, and it aired on TBN's *Praise the Lord* program. Notice some of the places that experienced snow.

- *China, India, Middle East*—Extremely cold, snowy winter reported by *USA Today* on March 7, 2008.[1]

- *Snow in Baghdad*—On January 11, 2008, CNN News reported the first snow in memory![2]

- *China snowfall*—On January 31, 2008, CNN.com reported that China was experiencing the worst snowfall in fifty years.[3]

- *Rare Middle East snowstorm*—The *New York Times* reported a Middle East snowstorm on January 31, 2008.[4]

- *North American blizzard of 2008*—A very powerful winter storm struck most of southern and eastern North America from March 6 to March 10, 2008, dumping record-breaking snowfall in the Ohio Valley and other northeast locations.[5]

- *Rare winter tornadoes across the South of the United States*—Rare winter tornadoes tore across the southern United States early in 2008.[6]

Through prophetic revelation, the Lord also ministered that there would be a sign to the Midwest coming through an earthquake that would take place. This was given to reveal that the powers of hell and political demonic strongholds were being shaken. The prophecy was as follows:

- *Shakings of the soil* (September 20, 2007)—The Spirit of God says that very soon in this nation you shall begin to feel the soil of this nation shake. For it shall be shaken upon the West, it shall be shaken in the middle, and it shall be shaken upon the East.

Here is what the news reported about it more than six months later:

A 5.4 earthquake early Friday rocked people awake as far away as Indiana, surprising residents unaccustomed to such a large Midwest temblor.[7]

Tremors were felt hundreds of miles away. We found reports from people who felt the quake in Kansas City, Chicago, St. Louis, Cincinnati, Madison, Wis., Des Moines and near Atlanta.[8]

We can see how God uses prophetic revelations to tell us key spiritual truths. Often the Lord will use natural events to reveal His prophetic plan that is about to unfold.

All of these different kinds of prophetic secrets are to reveal things from the Lord so we can see things from heaven's perspective and align our lives accordingly with His will. Whether it is a prophetic decree of blessing, prophetic announcement, prophetic direction, prophetic warning, or prophetic revelation, we need to welcome each one and begin to expect them to manifest in our own lives and in the world around us. We need to become tuned into them and accustomed to them so we can stay abreast of what God is doing.

CONDITIONS FOR PROPHETIC SECRETS

With prophetic secrets come certain conditions that cause these secrets to be fulfilled. Without fulfilling certain conditions and requirements, God's prophetic plans can be hindered or even aborted. When we receive a secret from the Lord, it is critical that we align ourselves with the word of the Lord. Let's look at some of the different conditions that enable and help the prophetic word to come to pass in our lives.

The prophetic needs to be coupled with prayer

You cannot have one without the other. When a prophecy is received, its fulfillment is not automatic. This is where so many people end up frustrated. They think just because they received a prophecy from God they have no responsibility to bring that word into manifestation. No, it must be coupled with prayer. When Elijah the prophet prophesied that it would not rain for three and a half years, it still required prayer for his prophecy to come to pass. The Bible says he was a man just like you and me, and he *prayed earnestly* that it wouldn't rain. "The effective, fervent prayer of a righteous man avails much. Elijah was a man with a nature like ours, and he prayed earnestly that it would not rain; and it did not rain on the land for three years and six months" (James 5:16–17). From this verse we can see it wasn't just his prophecy but also his prayers that brought this word to pass.

We see the same scenario when he began to prophesy that the rain was returning. "Then Elijah said to Ahab, 'Go up, eat and drink; for there is the sound of abundance of rain.' So Ahab went up to eat and drink. And Elijah went up to the top of Carmel; then he bowed down on the ground, and put his face between his knees" (1 Kings 18:41–42). Once again, you can see that not only did he prophesy rain, but he also prayed for the rain!

We see this example of prayer and prophecy with Anna. She was so dedicated to prayer and fasting concerning the coming of the Messiah that she fasted and prayed daily in the temple (Luke 2:37).

The prophetic word must be coupled with obedience

When a prophetic secret is given to us that we know is from God, we need to be obedient to any instructions included in that word. If there are not any specific instructions, then we should make sure we are living in obedience to God in general. I once knew a businessman who received numerous prophecies that he would have a successful business. Later, it was so frustrating to see him file bankruptcy and have to sell his business. However, it was revealed later that he was committing secret sin. He admitted that he thought his lifestyle was not an issue and that this word would happen *no matter what his choices were*. Disobedience can abort the word of the Lord.

Another businessman I knew had quit his business and gone to work for another company, but that company did not deal with him in integrity. I prophesied to him that the Lord would restore his previous business and, as a sign, God would prosper him but the other company would eventually fold due to their lack of integrity. The Lord even revealed the exact month and day the other company would go out of business. Of course, it was not our hope that the company would fold; God was simply speaking it to be a fact.

For some time it didn't seem the word was accurate, because this man couldn't seem to get his business going and struggled financially. It truly seemed like the word wasn't going to happen. The man began to doubt the word of the Lord. I reminded him that he needed to forgive that other company and make sure he was doing all the right things to be in biblical obedience so God's prophetic plan of restoring his business would come to pass. Because he stayed obedient to God through right choices and forgiveness, God turned his situation around and restored his business. The previous company that dealt with him deceitfully folded just as the word said. His obedience caused the word of the Lord to come to pass.

The prophetic word must be tested

Remember, there are three sources from which *prophetic* words can originate. Hopefully, they are directly from God, and that is what we always want to receive. However, at times people will prophesy something that is simply a word from the person's own heart, and it didn't come from God. This can get people off track if we are not wise in our response.

There are rare occasions when people have spoken under the influence of an evil spirit. We shouldn't live in fear of that, because typically that will not be the case, especially in a good church environment. However, we should test every word of prophecy, just as we test the preaching we hear for biblical soundness. There are three main ways to test a prophetic secret or prophecy.

- *It must agree with the Bible.* We should be able to find scriptures that give support and validity to the prophecy.

- *It must be discerned in our own spirit.* The prophecy should have a *right* feeling when you hear it. Even if the prophecy brought a degree of admonishment or conviction, you should be able to sense in your heart that it is from God.

- *It must be tested through wise counsel by others.* It is important to take the words we receive and test them against the
  wise counsel of our pastors, leaders, and unbiased godly
  resources who are there to tell us not what we want to hear
  but what we need to hear.

When we hear prophecy, it may not always be the thing we wanted
God to say. You may not find yourself jumping for joy when it is spoken.
In other cases, you may receive a word that pumped you up in your
soul and got you all excited, but the word wasn't from God. This is why
properly testing prophecy is needed. Of course, coupling prophecy with
prayer, as I said above, will only help you increase your discernment
when testing prophecy.

When Elisha prophesied to Naaman the leper, Naaman was angry
at a prophetic word that he didn't realize would eventually lead to his
healing. "And Elisha sent a messenger to him, saying, 'Go and wash in
the Jordan seven times, and your flesh shall be restored to you, and you
shall be clean'" (2 Kings 5:10). The problem was that Naaman wanted
to work the prophecy out on his terms, and he didn't feel he needed to
dip in a muddy river. There will be times when you will feel that way
too when the word of the Lord comes to you. That is why you have to
test the word and not rely on your own preferences or expectations as
Naaman did.

Instead of testing the word, some people want to manipulate it. What
do I mean by that? Some people will purposely take from the word what
they wanted to hear. It is funny how two people can hear the same
prophecy and come away with two entirely different interpretations of
it. One can hear it in a prideful way and jump ahead of God while the
other hears it through rejection and feels like the word is wrong because
he or she is not worthy enough! You can see why we have to test the
word and not rely solely on our own feelings.

At times when I ministered a prophetic word, the people receiving
were like Naaman, who didn't like parts of the prophecy. Afterward,

they want me to explain the prophecy to them. Their purpose for it is often motivated out of the desire to manipulate the prophecy because they didn't like something that was said. I find they usually are trying to accept some of the word and eliminate other parts. Naaman was angry, but thank God he accurately discerned the word and coupled it with obedience, which led to his healing.

The prophetic word must be coupled with faith. When a prophetic secret is revealed that we know is from the Lord, we need to mix faith with it. "For we also have had the gospel preached to us, just as they did; but the message they heard was of no value to them, because those who heard did not combine it with faith" (Hebrews 4:2, NIV). We can see from this verse that the word preached didn't benefit them because it wasn't mixed with the faith of those who heard it. This same principle is true with the prophetic words that come from the Holy Spirit. When the prophetic word was spoken to Mary concerning the birth of the Messiah, she said, "Let it be to me according to your word" (Luke 1:38). She didn't doubt it, but she acted on it by faith and expected it to come to pass. She believed in the word so strongly that she even traveled a distance to tell her aunt Elizabeth that she was pregnant with the Messiah!

On the other hand, the children of Israel received the prophetic word about a Promised Land, but they refused to embrace it with true faith. They allowed circumstances and challenges to douse their faith. As a result, because of unbelief, murmuring, and complaining, that generation of Israelites didn't see that prophetic word come to pass. They acted and responded in unbelief. They chose to believe their situation over the prophetic promise. Many died in the wilderness of their trials.

This is why many Christians don't see the word of the Lord come to pass but end up *dying in their trials*, so to speak. They can't respond to the word of the Lord in faith whether it is for their own personal life, for others, or for cities and nations.

The prophecy must be coupled with the right environment

We need to learn how to nurture the word received so it has the right environment to grow. The Bible likens the word, whether the written or spoken word, to a seed. When you receive a prophecy, it starts as a seed, and it needs nourishment, watering, and protection. I like to call this process *knowing how to hold on to the word of the Lord*. The Bible says that Satan comes immediately to steal the *seed* of the word, whether a seed from the Scriptures or those spoken by the Holy Spirit. "The sower sows the word. And these are the ones by the wayside where the word is sown. When they hear, Satan comes immediately and takes away the word that was sown in their hearts" (Mark 4:14–15). Satan will do the exact same thing in our lives. He uses the weakness of some who are not being rooted and grounded in the Word of God or a local church, choking the prophetic word from their lives through persecution, affliction, the cares of this world, deceitful riches, and lusts of other things, just as Jesus mentions in this parable.

As a result, people let go of the seed of that word, and it can't grow. Then they are often left scratching their heads when it doesn't bear fruit or come to pass. When that happens, many people blame the prophecy, the messenger, or even God. We need to learn how to hold on to the prophetic word by keeping it at the forefront of our thinking. We can do this by praying over it, talking about it, acting on it, and adding faith. Keep holding on to it and nourishing it, and the word will come to pass!

My wife and I received many words about our call to ministry. But I can tell you that in between those prophecies and seeing them come to pass were a lot of challenges. We had to hold on to those words because many days it looked as though they would never bear any fruit. We had to war over them and work it. No matter the obstacles that seemed thrown at us that were trying to get us to doubt and quit, we held on to what we believed and nourished those words so they could bear fruit in our lives.

The prophecy needs to be coupled with proper spiritual warfare

Warring over your prophecy is slightly different than just holding on to it and giving it the right spiritual environment. Warfare involves chasing out the enemy. When the enemy comes to steal it from you, you need to resist and chase him away from your property or prophecy. Tell him, "Hands off, in Jesus's name!" When you realize that there is an enemy who wants to destroy your prophecy, it will cause you to rise up and war. In 1 Timothy 1:18, we are told to wage a good warfare concerning the prophecies that we have received. We can hold faith and a good conscience and avoid shipwreck. Many prophetic secrets revealed have been shipwrecked because of the failure of people to fight for them to come to pass.

For example, when Herod heard that a ruler would come out of Bethlehem, he made plans to kill the prophetic word by ordering all male children two years of age and younger to be killed (Matthew 2:16). Of course, Jesus escaped while all the other babies were murdered. The devil will do all he can to destroy the word of the Lord. We have to war against him, pray, and resist his evil schemes so those words cannot be stolen from our hands.

In 2007 I prophesied that the hostages who had been held for many years in the nation of Colombia would be released. However, some time had passed, no updates were given, and it didn't seem like anything was happening. I know many people who warred in prayer for their release. Still, there had been no talk of a release at all. Many people continued to war in prayer that the prophecy would come to pass, especially those in my own church. Suddenly in the spring of 2008 they were released alive, as the prophecy said.

On another occasion in early 2008, the war was mounting between Venezuela and Colombia. Troops were moving in on the border between the two nations. During a prayer service at a church where I was ministering, the Lord had me decree with the people against the war. We prayed intently that the war would be aborted. Then God had me tell the people prophetically that if we would pray, then God would intervene within twenty-four hours, and in less than twenty-one days this war would be brought to a close.

The very next day the president of Venezuela announced that they would not go to war. The conflict fell, even though less than twenty-one days earlier it had looked very serious. Many groups around the world, and especially in those countries, had been praying earnestly. In the end, while my example is only one of many, the prophetic word coupled with spiritual warfare helped bring this good outcome to pass.

The prophetic word has to be coupled with right timing

When we receive a prophetic word, we must remember there are timing issues involved. Timing is the one area where prophets and prophetic people miss it the most. I am sure that many prophets in the Bible probably thought their prophecies were going to happen in their own lifetimes, but many of them didn't. We often want to determine the time frame for fulfillment of the prophecies we hear, so we grow weary in well doing, make wrong assumptions, or work overtime to try to make it happen.

We have to be wise about timing when we receive or hear a word. When it doesn't look like it is going to happen, it may be an issue of timing, not that the prophecy isn't true. It requires patience and keen discernment. I have experienced many occasions when I wanted certain prophecies in my life to manifest now! Yet, some of them were fulfilled years after when I expected them to.

Looking back now on how the Lord timed them, I am so grateful that they weren't fulfilled prematurely. They were fulfilled at the time I most needed them, not when I most wanted them. Be sensitive to the timing of God, and don't allow yourself to become frustrated because things didn't manifest when you expected. Otherwise, you may abort a wonderful prophetic promise over your life.

I have received prophetic words about political events and elections that I thought were meant for a certain election or season, but it turned out they were for another year and another time frame. Make sure you watch for God's timing when hearing the secrets of the Lord, and don't place wrong assumptions about timing on God's prophetic words.

MEETING PROPHETIC CONDITIONS

Meeting prophetic conditions is so important, and I cannot emphasize it enough. In an earlier chapter, I stated that people often say that a sign of a true prophet or prophecy is that the prophecy has to come to pass. However, we learned that isn't always the case. Many of the prophecies of the Bible prophets have yet to come to pass, even to this very day! Most of the time, we completely ignore certain conditions that must be met. However, if we don't properly align ourselves by meeting certain conditions, the prophecy may never come to pass, and it would have had nothing to do with the one who delivered it.

This happened once when I prophesied in a conference about a presidential election in a particular foreign nation. It appeared that a prophecy I gave didn't come to pass. I described the candidate whom I believed the Lord was choosing. At the time I prophesied it, I had never been to this nation and knew nothing about those who were running for office.

Then the Lord began to give me specific things the people were to watch for as the candidates were brought before the nation. The candidate I spoke about in the prophecy quickly became the front-runner and took the immediate lead in the polls. Many Christians began to support him and even sent him some of the things I prophesied about him winning the election. It looked like a clear win for him. However, along the way, just a few weeks before the final election, he decided to add a new campaign manager.

When it appeared that he would be a definite win and everything in the prophecy would come to pass, this campaign manager declared publicly that they didn't need God or any prophet who spoke about this election to win. This message was reported in the newspapers and on television all over the country. The manager felt that the credit for the win should be his. He was overconfident because he had helped other candidates win. His public words terribly offended the Christian community, which was supporting the candidate. Yes, you guessed it, because of those statements, the candidate lost because the people would not vote for him.

I am convinced that the prophecy was conditional, based on his actions. The loss shook the candidate, who later repented for making such a great mistake. He immediately made plans to correct his error and run again. He made a public statement to his nation as to why he lost, and many regained faith in his acknowledgement of God.

Often what appears to be an unconditional prophecy is still dependent on our actions. This is why you cannot assume that a prophecy was false. We don't always know the facts. I believe this man's choices aborted God's intended plan, even though the prophecy sounded like it was a done deal. Prophecy is conditional upon our actions. Our disobedience, attitudes, words, and actions can affect the prophetic words from coming to pass in our lives. When we don't align ourselves with the prophecy, we may never see it manifest. We find many examples in the Bible where a prophecy appeared unconditional, but because people either repented or refused to align with the prophecy, the outcome was different from the original prophecy.

The prophecy of Scripture itself cannot be changed, and it will happen as it has been written. However, we do find many prophecies spoken in the Bible that didn't turn out the way they were spoken. Of course, some of these have yet to come to pass, but others were fulfilled, and the outcomes were different from how it was prophesied—even in the case of some of the most revered prophets of Scripture.

For example, look at Jeremiah 18:7–10:

> The instant I speak concerning a nation and concerning
> a kingdom, to pluck up, to pull down, and to destroy

> it, if that nation against whom I have spoken turns from its evil, I will relent of the disaster that I thought to bring upon it. And the instant I speak concerning a nation and concerning a kingdom, to build and to plant it, if it does evil in My sight so that it does not obey My voice, then I will relent concerning the good with which I said I would benefit it.

Notice that the things the Lord prophesied were conditional on the people's actions. Prophecies spoken over individuals, cities, nations, and churches about future events are conditional upon our actions, attitudes, prayer, obedience, and faith.

Jonah the prophet gave a harsh word of judgment against the city of Nineveh. He told them that the city would be judged in forty days: "And Jonah began to enter the city on the first day's walk. Then he cried out and said, 'Yet forty days, and Nineveh shall be overthrown!'" (Jonah 3:4).

God didn't even indicate that there was anything they could do to stop this impending disaster. Yet this word didn't come to pass exactly as it was prophesied. We find later that it was conditional upon the repentance of those who dwelt in Nineveh. This response of repentance from the people of Nineveh was never mentioned in the prophecy of Jonah as an option. In fact, the king of Nineveh proclaimed a fast in hopes that God would change His mind (verses 7–9). We know that God did accept their repentance, and Nineveh was spared. I am sure that some thought that Jonah missed it because his prophecy had said specifically that the city would be overthrown in *forty days*...end of story. Well, it never happened! They repented, and this prophecy, first spoken by Jonah, was *changed* based on the actions of the people.

In another example, the Lord sent a prophet to speak what appeared to be an unconditional prophecy for the house of Eli. However, because Eli and his two sons became corrupt, they aborted what God had originally said over them. "Therefore the LORD God of Israel says: 'I said indeed that your house and the house of your father would walk before Me forever.' But now the LORD says: 'Far be it from Me; for those who honor Me I will honor, and those who despise Me shall be lightly esteemed. Behold, the days are coming that I will cut off your arm and the arm of your father's house, so that there will not be an old man in your house'" (1 Samuel 2:30–31). In spite of previous prophetic promises that Eli and his sons would inherit the priesthood, the present actions interrupted it. God had even originally said, "Indeed," indicating that it would happen. Yet later we find God saying, "But now," meaning something happened in the meantime that interrupted God's original plan spoken by the prophet.

How about the prophecy that was given to King Hezekiah that he would die? There were no conditions or additional information that the prophet Isaiah gave him. The prophecy simply said, "Set your house in order, for you shall die" (Isaiah 38:1). However, the original prophecy seemed to change later because he set his face against the wall and prayed. As a result, the Lord granted him fifteen more years to live. Is it possible that many people in that day may have thought that Isaiah the prophet missed it? Those close to Hezekiah who may have heard or documented the original prophecy might have wondered what happened if they weren't privy to the updated prophecy that came after his repentance. If you remember, the original word was spoken without any conditions.

We also know that King Josiah was a powerful reformer, and God prophesied to him through a woman named Huldah. This prophetess spoke a prophetic word about King Josiah that he would die in peace because his heart was tender and he had humility toward God (2 Chronicles 34:28).

Yet, even though she prophesied that he would die in peace, from further reading of his life in Scripture, we know he died by the sword because he didn't seek the counsel of the Lord: "And the archers shot King Josiah; and the king said to his servants, 'Take me away, for I am severely wounded.' His servants therefore took him out of that chariot and put him in the second chariot that he had, and they brought him to Jerusalem. So he died, and was buried in one of the tombs of his fathers" (2 Chronicles 35:23–24). Was this prophetess false, or did she miss it? Or was this an example of conditional prophecy, which requires us to align with what was originally said?

Samuel the prophet prophesied that Saul would be king over Israel, which did happen (1 Samuel 9:17). Samuel also prophesied that Saul's kingdom would be established forever (1 Samuel 13:13). We know, however, that the Lord later said the kingdom would be literally ripped away from Saul (1 Samuel 15:26–28). This was a very different picture from what was originally prophesied. The prophecies spoken by Samuel were conditional upon King Saul's actions and obedience, even though these conditions were not mentioned when it was originally prophesied.

Another example of a prophecy that changed was the word given to King Ahab by Elijah that disaster was going to come upon him and upon his sons for the evil he had done. However, Ahab repented and humbled himself, so later God said he would not bring disaster upon him during his lifetime (1 Kings 21:19–29).

There are also what I call the "if" prophecies. They are prophetic conditions that require our involvement in the prophetic process. In other words, the condition and responsibility on our part is mentioned in the actual prophecy to help aid in the prophetic word coming to pass.

One example can be found in 2 Chronicles 7:14 (emphasis added):

> *If* My people who are called by My name will humble themselves, and pray and seek My face, and turn from their wicked ways, *then* I will hear from heaven, and will forgive their sin and heal their land.

Notice the responsibility expected by the addition of the word *if*. Based on *if* they do certain things, there is a result. It is *then* and only then that the prophetic promise comes to pass. In other words, if they would do their part in the prophetic secret, then God would do His.

By now you can probably see that meeting conditions and aligning ourselves with the word of the Lord is so important. What I want you to see is that we need to align ourselves with the prophetic word of the Lord so we can enjoy blessing. Once we know a word is from the Lord, we must make sure we align with it, whether conditions were spoken in the prophecy or not. The ultimate goal is that we want to receive the secrets of the Lord and walk out the things intended by God for our good and not allow that to be aborted.

Be Encouraged

As I close this book, I want you to be deeply encouraged about the prophetic things of God. See them as a blessing that you can operate in and also receive from. As you embrace them, my prayer is that you will come away knowing how to exercise your spiritual senses to hear, see, and perceive more accurately. I pray you have learned some truths to help you realize your prophetic potential and to enable you to operate in the right protocol, boundaries, and responsibilities that go with the secrets of the Lord. It has been my desire that the proper balance and guidelines that I have discussed in these pages will aid in your prophetic destiny.

As you learn to draw from the prophetic anointing in your spirit, keep your life submitted to the right spiritual oversight, and allow God to teach you every day. God wants to use you to share His secrets to the world. We need to be prepared and willing to let all creation know that the Revealer of secrets has come. Yes, my friend, this is truly great news!

PRAYER OF SALVATION

—•— ⊨◊⊨ —•—

I WANT TO PERSONALLY INVITE YOU TO ACCEPT JESUS CHRIST as your personal Savior and Lord if you don't already know Him. Simply pray the following prayer with all your heart and faith:

Heavenly Father, I come to You in the name of Jesus. The Bible says whoever will call on the name of the Lord will be saved (Acts 2:21). I now call upon You, Jesus, and ask You to come into my heart and my life according to Romans 10:9–10, which says that if I will confess with my mouth the Lord Jesus and believe in my heart that You, God, raised Him from the dead, I would be saved.

I therefore believe in my heart that You, God, did raise Jesus from the dead, and I now say with my mouth that Jesus is my Lord! I ask You, Lord, to forgive me of all my sins, and I know that I am now a new creation in Christ Jesus (2 Corinthians 5:17; 1 John 1:9).

BAPTISM OF THE HOLY SPIRIT

+·+ ⋈◊⋈ +·+

NOW THAT YOU KNOW YOU ARE A CHRISTIAN AND PRAYED THE prayer of salvation, or you already accepted Jesus, then you are ready to be filled with His Holy Spirit. Pray this prayer:

Heavenly Father, I know that I am saved. Jesus is my Lord, and I believe He is alive and that You raised Him from the dead. You promised in Your Word to give me the Holy Spirit if I would ask you (Luke 11:13). You also said I would receive power after the Holy Spirit comes upon me (Acts 1:8). I now ask You to fill me with the Holy Spirit. Holy Spirit, rise up within me. I ask You to fill me with Your Spirit, and, as I praise You, God, I will now begin to speak with tongues as You give me the utterance (Acts 2:4).

Begin to praise God for filling you with the Holy Spirit, and speak out the words and syllables not in your own language but in the language of the Holy Spirit with the syllables you are hearing inside your heart. Now use your own voice, lips, and tongue to speak. God's Spirit will give you the words. Your job is to yield to the words given by opening your mouth and speaking forth your new heavenly language.

Continue to pray in tongues every day!

Notes

CHAPTER 1
HEARING THRONE-ROOM SECRETS

1. "Disaster Management, Iran: Bam Earthquake," International Federation of Red Cross and Red Crescent Societies, http://www.ifrc.org/what/disasters/response/iran.asp (accessed March 23, 2009).

CHAPTER 2
THE REVEALER OF SECRETS HAS COME

1. Smith Wigglesworth, "Monday Morning Devotionals," http://www.geocities.com/mmdevotionals/44_operating_in_the_gifts_of_the_spirit.html (accessed March 25, 2009).

2. *Broadman and Holman Ultrathin Reference Edition* (Nashville, TN: B&H Publishing Group, 1996).

CHAPTER 4
LESSONS IN HEARING GOD'S SECRETS

1. Hank Kunneman, *Don't Leave God Alone* (Lake Mary, FL: Charisma House, 2008).

CHAPTER 9
ALIGNING YOURSELF WITH THE PROPHETIC WORD

1. Doyle Rice, "Record Snowfalls Mean Big Meltdown," *USA Today*, March 7, 2008, http://www.usatoday.com/weather/storms/winter/2008-03-06-winter_n.htm (accessed May 6, 2009).

2. Carol Jordan, "Let It Snow…in Baghdad," CNN.com, January 11, 2008, http://www.cnn.com/exchange/blogs/in.the.field/2008/01/let-it-snow-in-baghdad.html (accessed April 3, 2009).

3. "China advises millions to abandon travel plans," CNN.com, January 31, 2008, http://edition.cnn.com/2008/WORLD/asiapcf/01/31/china.weather/index.html (accessed April 3, 2009).

4. Agence France-Presse, "Middle East; Rare Snowstorm," NYTimes.com, January 31, 2008, http://query.nytimes.com/gst/fullpage.html?res=940CE4DD133EF932A05752C0A96E9C8B63&sec=&spon= (accessed April 3, 2009).

5. "North American Blizzard of 2008," Wikipedia.com, http://en.wikipedia.org/wiki/North_American_blizzard_of_2008 (accessed April 3, 2009). See related sources used by Wikipedia for more information.

6. Demian McLean, "Tornadoes in South Kill 50 in Rare Winter Strike," Bloomberg.com, http://www.bloomberg.com/apps/news?pid=20601103&sid=aJ9moCnc8_i8 (accessed April 3, 2009).

7. "5.4 Earthquake Rocks Illinois; Also Felt in Indiana," *The Associated Press*, April 18, 2008, http://www.herald-dispatch.com/homepage/x996192529 (accessed April 3, 2009).

8. Mike Carney, "Early Morning Earthquake Ripples Through the Middle of the Country," *USA Today*, http://blogs.usatoday.com/ondeadline/2008/04/early-morning-e.html (accessed April 3, 2009).

ONE VOICE MINISTRIES
The Ministry of Hank & Brenda Kunneman

Conferences

Hank and Brenda travel worldwide, ministering in churches, conferences, and conventions. They bring relevant biblical messages from a prophetic viewpoint, and their dynamic preaching style is coupled with the demonstrations of the Holy Spirit. Though they preach at events separately, they are especially known for their unique platform of ministry together as a team in the ministry of the gifts of the Spirit. For additional information about scheduling a ministry or church conference with Hank and/or Brenda, you may contact One Voice Ministries at 402.896.6692, or you may request a ministry packet online at www.ovm.org

Books, Products, and Resources

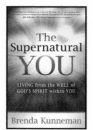

Books, audio, and video materials are available at the Kunnemans' online store at www.ovm.org. Book titles include *The Supernatural You*, *The Revealer of Secrets*, *When Your Life Has Been Tampered With*, *Hide and Seek*, *Don't Leave God Alone*, and *Chaos in the King's Court*. The One Voice Ministries' Web site also provides many ministry resources, including Hank's page called "Prophetic Perspectives" that provides excerpts and prophetic insight on world events. Brenda's page, "The Daily Prophecy," has changed lives around the world. There are also numerous articles for study.

Lord of Hosts Church

Hank and Brenda Kunneman also pastor Lord of Hosts Church in Omaha, Nebraska. Filled with captivating praise and worship and sound, prophetic teaching, services at Lord of Hosts Church are always rich with the presence of God. Lord of Hosts Church is known for its solid team of leaders, organized style and ministry that touches the everyday needs of people. Through the many avenues of ministry the church is raising up strong believers. Many ministries worldwide have referred to Lord of Hosts Church to be among the most up-and-coming, cutting-edge churches in the United States. For further information about Lord of Hosts Church, call 402.896.6692 or visit online at www.lohchurch.org or www.ovm.org.

Pastors Hank and Brenda Kunneman
Lord of Hosts Church and One Voice Ministries

5351 S. 139th Plaza
Omaha, Nebraska 68137

Phone: (402) 896-6692
Fax: (402) 894-9068

www.ovm.org
www.lohchurch.org

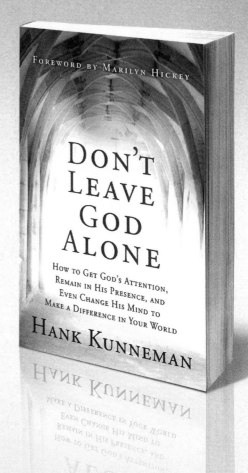